Acclaim for BUSHCRAFT

'If Ray Mears isn't a Great Living Englishman, then goodness me, who is? The man is great, and he doesn't even begin to know how great he is. Ray is a persuader, pragmatist and populariser in the Durrell–Attenborough-Bellamy tradition.' – Robert Crampton, *The Times Magazine*

'Complete – and certainly aesthetically pleasing . . . it is sure to consolidate Mears' position as the foremost purveyor of bushcraft in the UK today.' – *Geographical Magazine*

'Ray Mears is a bushman first and foremost and really can survive in any extreme environment. I can't think of a better companion in a crisis.' – Tim Lewis, GQ

'By paragraph three of the intro you are itching to throw off the shackles of civilised life and plant your feet in the wilderness. If ever a book was calculated to invoke the call of the wild, this is it.' – *Live Wire*

'This is more than just a survival manual: the well-written text and illustrations will appeal as much to the armchair wayfarer as the committed explorer. As well as his bushcraft ability and communication skills, one of Mears' strengths is his sensitive appreciation of the environment and his understanding of other, indigenous cultures. All these virtues shine through in this illuminating book.' – *Good Book Guide*

Dedication

For all the students of bushcraft who have attended Woodlore courses. You have been the greatest teachers: watching you tackle this vast and complex subject has been inspiring to one who has walked this path so long.

AUTHOR'S NOTE

This smaller format edition of BUSHCRAFT has been prepared in response to numerous requests for a more portable version of the book. We've taken this opportunity to cut out non-essential text and correct any typographical errors that appeared in the hardback. In the Outfit chapter we've also been able to include a few new photographs of kit that wasn't available when the hardback was published.

My thanks to all of you who've been in contact to offer comments and suggestions about my book. Remember, the essence of bushcraft is not mere survival, but to be at one with nature.

I hope ESSENTIAL BUSHCRAFT will enable you to reach that state.

Ray Mears, March 2003

ESSENTIAL BUSHCRAFT

Ray Mears

Illustrations by Ben McNutt

Hodder & Stoughton

Text and photographs copyright © 2002 by Ray Mears
Illustrations © 2002 by Ben McNutt

First published in Great Britain in 2003 by Hodder & Stoughton
A division of Hodder Headline

A Hodder & Stoughton book

19

A CIP catalogue record for this title is available from the British Library

ISBN 13: 9780340829714

Book design by Janette Revill

Printed and bound in Italy by Graphicom Srl

Hodder & Stoughton
A division of Hodder Headline
338 Euston Road
London NW1 3BH

CONTENTS

PREFACE

BY EWAN MACGREGOR

There I was, standing in the rain trying to make a shelter in the middle of the Honduran jungle, when a thought came to me: why am I doing this? The answer: Ray Mears. When I was asked if I wanted to go and make a television programme about how I would cope with a week in the rainforest, my immediate reaction was 'No!' Then they told me who I would be going with, and I changed my answer to 'Well maybe'.

Like most of us, I only knew about Ray Mears from his television series where he makes fires and shelters as if by magic. Let me tell you that what you see on screen is only a tiny part of what Ray and *Bushcraft* are about. When you're with Ray you not only learn some amazing skill (and, yes, it is possible to do them on your own) but you also learn a lot about yourself. There was one moment while we were in Honduras when I just lost it. I was wet, I was freezing cold and I wanted to go home that minute.

I stormed off into the forest on my own, slashing at anything and everything with my panga.

When I came back, Ray just asked me if I'd found any of the twenty-odd varieties of seriously poisonous snake that live there and suggested that if I had been bitten that would have been it, because there was no way they could have got me out of the jungle before I died. Point taken, Ray, I just hadn't thought it through.

Only a few of us will ever be lucky enough to experience Ray's wonderfully enabling ideas and skills at first hand, so I'm very pleased that he's found the time to explore and explain some of them in this book. Whether you're going into the outback

tomorrow or just fancy a weekend camping in the garden you'll learn from *Bushcraft*.

I just wish I'd had a copy before I went to Honduras . . .

INTRODUCTION

'*We learned that one cannot defy nature, but must adapt and accommodate oneself to her. Nature will not change; it is man who must change, if he is to live in conditions where nature is dominant.*'

Knut Haukelid *Skis Against the Atom*

Bushcraft is the term I employ to describe a deeper knowledge of the wild and of nature. It is a huge tree that branches out in many directions to botany, zoology, craft work, outdoors leadership and countless other divisions. At its root, though, is reliance upon oneself and on nature. In the study of bushcraft we step beyond survival and learn the subtlety that makes outdoor life both certain and enjoyable. Everyone who visits wild places will benefit from bushcraft knowledge. What could be more natural than to recognise the wild things around us and find food, shelter, fire and water?

I do not wish, though, to suggest that we should turn our backs on the skills and tools of today. Far from it – my hope is that we shall learn to use our modern tools more wisely by bolstering them with wisdom from the past. Bushcraft ties us closely to nature, and at its core is respect for nature and all living things.

Bushcraft is not necessarily easily learned – many of the skills will challenge us to dig deep inside ourselves and discover hidden toughness and resilience that our modern life rarely demands of us. Rising to these challenges develops determination, a positive mental attitude and an increased liveliness of spirit.

The great difficulty in writing about bushcraft is the sheer scale of the task, so I have confined myself to the fundamental skills. I have assumed that the reader is already interested in travelling in wilderness, can navigate and is conversant with first aid techniques. My aim is to describe the most important skills or the most versatile.

Knowledge is invisible and weighs nothing. Be mindful that in times of crisis if you can find shelter in the forest, rub sticks for fire and know which wild plants around you can be eaten you will have a home, hearth and a meal.

OUTFIT

'I learned how much of what we think to be necessary is superfluous; I learned how few things are essential, and how essential those things really are.'

Bernard Ferguson, *Chindits, Burma 1943*.

• •

When putting together a suitable outfit for wilderness travel, the golden rule is K I S S – Keep It Simple, Stupid. You will not need anything elaborate, easily broken or complicated. Your outfit should be adaptable according to the climate and the nature of the activities you are to undertake.

At its most basic this is what you will need:

- something to carry your outfit in
- something to sleep under
- something to sleep in
- something to sleep on
- navigational equipment
- something to cook over
- something cook in
- something to carry water
- a mug
- eating utensils
- food
- medical kit
- illumination at night
- wash kit
- odds and ends to make life comfortable – 'possibles'
- clothing

SOMETHING TO CARRY YOUR OUTFIT IN

For short overnight hikes, a large day sack of 35 litres volume will be adequate. For more extended journeys, a medium-sized pack of 55-60 litres volume will be large enough in hot climates where you will need less clothing and a lighter sleeping-bag. For cold weather take a 100 litre rucksack or larger.

If you are canoeing you will need a day sack with a large canoe pack, which should be fitted with straps to enable you to carry it as if it were a rucksack. There are two choices: the traditional canvas Duluth sack, or the more modern dry bag with rucksack strap attachments. For canoeing I prefer the Duluth sack; for whitewater rafting, the dry bag.

I prefer rucksacks to have only one main compartment without any division: this reduces the zips and seams, making for a stronger rucksack. I like there to be several

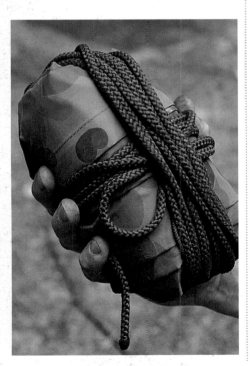

large outside pockets for water-bottles, water-purification equipment, first-aid kit, torch and lunch, etc.

SOMETHING TO SLEEP UNDER

The most versatile shelter is the simple tarp or fly-sheet. I favour the Australian Army hoochi, which is well equipped with attachment points and made to a high standard. I pack my tarp up with guy lines and suspension lines attached, then fold it neatly so that when I come to put it up after dark there are no tangles. When making a more fixed camp I use a larger canvas tarp set over a ridge pole or over a length of rope stretched tightly between two trees.

As the temperature drops, thermally efficient shelters are more appropriate, such as hiking or mountain tents. The Hilleberg, a Swedish-manufactured tent, is made to a high standard, with superb ventilation.

A tent is also preferable in tropical conditions or where insects and/or snakes are hazardous, or where there are few trees to string a mosquito net or a fly-sheet. The Australian Mozzie Dome has two flexible poles that cross to create a double hoop that stretches taut a fine mosquito net, which is sealed to an integral ground sheet. A lightweight fly-sheet can be attached over this with another pole.

Of tent designs my favourite is the Scandinavian one-pole tepee Kota or Laavu, as used in the far north of Scandinavia. The advantage of tepees is that in winter or inclement weather you can stay warm and cook inside them and they are easily illuminated with candles.

Opposite top right: Tarp shelters are airy and enable you to observe nature on all sides.

Opposite centre: Hilleberg Keron 3GT – an excellent tent for two to three people. Inset: Good ventilation reduces condensation problems.

Opposite bottom: Lightweight nylon tepee – light enough to be carried for solo camping, yet large enough to sleep in comfort.

SOMETHING TO SLEEP IN

Your sleeping-bag is one of the most important items of your equipment so choose it carefully. Avoid sleeping-bags that have not been designed for specifically outdoor use.

Your sleeping-bag should fit you well: before you buy it, get into it and make sure that it is both long and wide enough, that you can move around in it freely, and that there is room for your clothes and boots if you are going to be in cold conditions: it is normal practice to store them overnight in your sleeping-bag – otherwise they may freeze. Choose a

sleeping-bag suitable for the temperature range you are likely to encounter. Season ratings are unreliable as no universal standard applies. Choose a sleeping-bag that is likely to be too warm, rather than the reverse: you can always undo the zip, if need be, and use it as a duvet.

A sleeping-bag must also be fitted with an integral hood and, for Arctic conditions, a baffle that closes around your shoulders and prevents you breathing moisture into the bag, which reduces insulation.

In very hot climates I tend to use a poncho liner – a thin lightweight blanket used by the US military to insulate the military poncho.

In hot, arid climates, with vehicles, a swag or a bed roll is commonly used. This is a canvas case containing a 5-cm thick foam mattress, a small duvet and a pillow. It's excellent for sleeping out under the stars.

Sales assistants devote much time to discussing the relative merits of sleeping-bag stuffing materials. They usually argue that down is lightweight when it is packed but if it gets wet it stays wet and you get cold; synthetic materials are slightly heavier and bulkier, but retain warmth when damp. This argument is all true, but once any sleeping-bag is wet it ceases to provide adequate insulation. When I am in the high Arctic I prefer a down sleeping-bag because there is less risk that it will become moist, it packs up small, it weighs little and gives good warmth. When I am in temperate climates I use a synthetic sleeping-bag because it is better in damp conditions, but I ensure that I keep it dry.

The efficiency of all sleeping-bags can be improved if used with a Gore-tex bivvy bag. Ex-military ones are ideal. If you put a good-quality sleeping-bag with a sleeping mat inside a Gore-tex bivvy bag you have a lightweight bed roll. The bivvy bag protects you from draughts and breezes, so is particularly useful when sleeping under a tarp.

When you carry your sleeping-bag make sure it is protected from moisture: either stuff it into a dry bag, or pack it into a bin-liner, inside the stuff sack.

Above left: Woodlore 'Golden Eagle' – a sleeping bag with a central zip, making it more practical for long-term use.

Above right: Poncho liners are light and versatile, and dry out quickly.

SOMETHING TO SLEEP ON

A sleeping mat is a vital item. While it is possible to improvise beds efficiently from natural materials it is far easier to use either a closed-cell foam mattress or Thermarest mat, which is an open-cell mattress within an impervious envelope, which can be inflated so it is a cross between an air-bed and a foam mattress. It blocks the transmission of heat from your body to the ground. Trying to sleep outdoors without ground insulation or one of these is misery. In the far north, spruce boughs are still widely used under a foam mat to provide a good depth of insulation.

NAVIGATIONAL EQUIPMENT

The compass is the key to the wilderness, with your map, but you may also need other navigational equipment. Before your journey, your planning will tell you what maps you need and the nature of the terrain you will cross.

Order or purchase maps in the most suitable scale for the area to which you are going. Ideally the scale should be 1:50,000 or 1:25,000, but in some parts of the world the only maps available may be 1:500,000.

Your maps should be protected from moisture: Keep them well stashed inside your rucksack, wrapped in waterproof zip-lock bags. The map in current use should be protected inside a map case.

Your compass is a precision tool and must be carefully chosen and protected. For the wilderness sighting compasses are ideal. The Silva compass type 54 or type 15 TDCL is perhaps the most popular one in use today and for good reason: the type 54 provides a very accurate sighting of bearings using a lens system while the type 15 provides a sighting using a mirror and is rather more robust because the mirror cover folds to protect the needle housing. Regardless of which compass you choose it must be kept in a case. I keep mine in a top jacket pocket. When travelling by aircraft I ensure that my compass travels as hand luggage and thus is protected from pressure differences, which may cause a bubble to appear in the liquid-filled needle housing.

Remember that for navigation you will also need a waterproof-paper notebook and soft B pencil to record daily your route, the bearings on which you have marched and grid references. This gives you the chance to check whether you have made a mistake and, if so, retrace your route. This is crucial in wild country where there are few landmarks or features, especially in rainforest.

The global positioning system, or GPS, is having a major impact on outdoor pursuits. No bigger than a mobile phone, it can receive transmissions from a series of orbiting satellites and triangulate its position with great accuracy. The Garmin e-trex Summit also provides an electronic compass and altimeter, which enables you to predict weather trends, take sightings, locate yourself and plot your journey.

GPS is not an alternative to a map and compass: any electronic device is prone to damage, battery failure or weather damage.

Left: Key to the wilderness - Silva Type 15TDCL compass.

Right: Silva Type 54 compass.

COOKING EQUIPMENT

Depending on the nature of your journey, how light you wish to travel and the climate in which you are travelling, you will need to take with you suitable pans, and perhaps a stove: either a pocket-sized military tommy cooker, which burns solid fuel tablets made of hexamine, or a methylated-spirits-fired trangia, or perhaps a pressure petrol stove.

Camelbak 3 litre with a drinking straw has become an essential item; Dromedary 4 litre is very strong and flexible; standard NATO 1 litre flask.

Optimus Nova – pressure petrol stove.

WATER CARRIERS, MUGS, EATING AND FOOD

A water carrier is not necessary in areas where there is a lot of water, but everywhere else it is of critical importance. I prefer the strong army canteen: I use two one-litre British Army water bottles, which are strong and reliable. These are made of black plastic and protect the water, which may have been purified with iodine, from degrading in sunlight. In addition, I often carry a four-quart collapsible water canteen, which I fill towards the end of the day. In deserts I increase the number of two-quart canteens to ensure I have a minimum of six litres of water contained in vessels with me.

A drinking cup or mug is important: most practical is a metal military mug or cup, particularly the stainless-steel ones which are graduated to enable you to judge liquid volumes when cooking and can serve as a cooking pot. The lid will keep off flies and other insects. All stainless-steel utensils can be heated over a stove or fire to sterilise them.

You will also need a spoon, but a fork is not essential. You can buy titanium or plastic spoons in any outdoors shop.

Food for the trail must be carefully packed to protect it from the weather and damp. If you are travelling in bear country, pack it so that it can be suspended from a tree, out of the reach of marauding claws.

MEDICAL KIT

If you are planning a wilderness trip and haven't had any first aid-training you should get some: in the wilderness, you may need to be able to do more than a first-aider in an urban situation. If you haven't done a course recently, you should attend one to refresh your memory. You may be days from professional medical assistance and must be able to deal with a wide range of problems and even make life-saving decisions. You will almost certainly have to treat and manage wounds.

The contents of your medical kit will be bound by space, weight restrictions and experience. Discuss with your GP the essentials for a long haul trip. You will need all or some of the following items.

- surgical gloves
- some antiseptic hand wipes

- a CPR barrier of some description – pocket mask or shield
- EMT shears or small scissors
- tweezers for removing splinters
- water-purification tablets, either chlorine or iodine tablets for use when irrigating wounds
- a sterile scalpel blade
- a needle for draining blisters
- a paper clip to reduce blood underneath a thumbnail
- a magnifying lens for removal of ticks or other insects from skin
- some gaffer tape to be wrapped around splints
- digital thermometer to read high and low temperatures

For long trips
- an emergency dental kit
- a notebook and pencil to record details of a condition, location and map reference, when sending someone for help

- forceps, for suturing, and sutures if qualified to use them
- a sam splint, in flexible aluminium
- a high-reading thermometer
- a low-reading thermometer, to check for hypothermia
- venom extractor and anti-venom, in areas with venomous snakes
- sterile liquids, for wound irrigation with a 20cc syringe with a green canula or steripod
- topical antiseptic such as Povidone Iodine in the form of Aqueous Betadene solution for bites, small lesions and minor cuts
- anti-microbial ointment for slow-healing wounds and ulcers
- aloe vera, for sunburn
- calamine lotion and hydrocortisone for burns

For blisters
- hydrocollide bandages for burst blisters – try

Compeed bandages which are perfect for the job
- mole foam and mole skin to prevent the rubbing at a hot spot in a boot

Bandages
- an assortment of adhesive bandages, such as 3M nexcore active strips which stay on; Leukostrips, Cover strips or Steri Strips to close a clean wound
- 5cm or 10cm square non-adherent gauze pads, Meloin pads or similar, for wound treatment and covering
- self-adhesive gauze pads
- a sterile trauma pad to apply pressure and help staunch bleeding.
- an elastic bandage, either 7.5cm crêpe, or adhesive coban bandage, if preferred, for sprains
- safety pins

ILLUMINATION
Lighting is important for dealing with emergencies at night. With my vehicle-portable camp, I carry pressure petrol lanterns which go into the vehicle last so that if I arrive at a campsite in the dark they are the first item to hand. Here, self-igniting lanterns have an advantage over those that must be primed and lit. Take with you some spare mantels.

Candles are still useful, particularly in tents which protect them from breezes and in the rainforest, where breezes are unusual: also head torches, such as the one made by Petzel. I like a small LED light, which I can wear around my neck, and a small handheld flashlight with a powerful halogen bulb, which is useful in rescue situations or emergencies.

WASH KIT
Keep your wash kit simple; avoid scented products, as they attract insects. I carry with me pine-tar soap and an antibacterial antiperspirant

Travel towels fold up small, are absorbent and dry rapidly anywhere except the tropics, where they don't dry and smell mouldy.

CLOTHING
Arid lands
Perhaps the easiest of all environments for which to dress. Wear woollen socks inside lightweight leather boots. Some of the best boots for these areas are to be found in Africa where comfortable flat-soled leather shoes are made for safari use, which are excellent for hiking through the bush. If these are not available, consider ex-military desert boots.

Underwear should be loose-fitting cotton. I like to wear shorts wherever possible, but you must have long trousers with you: to cover up against the sun and for protection in the evening from biting insects. The best way to avoid malaria and other diseases transmitted by insect bite, like dengue fever and scrub typhus, is to cover yourself in loose-fitting tightly woven fabrics.

As for tops, I wear a tightly woven cotton jacket/shirt, loose-fitting to vent moisture and give shade. Otherwise wear a T-shirt and a

Petzl Tikka head torch.

lightweight jacket, or a tightly woven cotton shirt. The jacket/shirt is harder wearing and survives longer in thorny country.

It is always a good idea to carry with you a pullover as it can be quite cold at night. You can wear it under a jacket/shirt for protection against wind. Bear in mind that in some areas, such as the North African desert, during

Lightweight leather safari boots.

winter temperatures can drop extremely low, and in these conditions I have taken a down jacket to keep warm at night.

One of the most important items of all is a hat to protect you from the sun: the stronger the sunlight the wider the brim is the old rule. I like the hats made by Akubra, who produce a felted hat of superior quality.

Wear sunglasses to reduce the effect of glare. A head net, kept in the top pocket of your shirt, discourages insects after dark.

Jungle

In the rainforest clothing has to withstand continuous wet. There is no better footwear than the US Army jungle boot: look for genuine boots in the modern version, which has Cordura uppers and leather soles with speedlacing. New boots will stretch a little after initial wearing. Inside I wear two pairs of wool socks. Wool doesn't go mouldy and unpleasant like cotton socks.

I prefer Lycra cycling shorts as underwear: they don't chafe between your legs. Wear long trousers, not shorts – strong ones that dry fast. Again the best are often ex-military trousers.

Try to avoid camouflage: in many countries you may be mistaken for a soldier and find yourself in trouble.

On top, a long-sleeved shirt or a jacket/shirt of tightly woven cotton gives good protection against insects and thorns. Make sure it has long sleeves, which can be rolled down in the evening to cover up and avoid mosquito bites.

I tend not to wear a hat when I'm hiking through the rainforest as the brim impedes my vision, causing me to bang my head on low branches and vines, but on river journeys a short-brimmed cotton jungle hat is essential.

US Army jungle boots.

Normally in the rainforest we have two sets of clothes: a dry set and a wet set. Your wet clothes are those you wear during the day. In the evening, after setting up camp, you change out of your wet clothes, wring them out and hang them up to dry, then put on your dry clothes, which are kept in a dry bag. Powder your feet when you take off your boots and put on a pair of lightweight sneakers to wear around camp. Pack them carefully before setting out the next day, when you will put on your wet clothes again.

Temperate

With four distinct seasons your dress may vary between everything from Arctic and arid, particularly during the spring. I like a good strong leather hiking boot that comes high up my leg. If you step into soft ground in short boots, they are swamped. I like a boot with a Gore-tex liner, but this is not essential as waterproof socks are available to prevent your feet becoming cold and moist. Further protection from rain is afforded by waterproof gaiters.

Wear two pairs of good wool socks and ex-military trousers but nothing too expensive: you may have to push through thorns and briars and your trousers will take a battering. If you are going far out on the trail, consider taking some tightly woven windproof trousers, such as those made of Ventile fabric for added protection.

I prefer cotton underwear but in these circumstances others wear cycling shorts or even swimming trunks.

Conventional wisdom suggests that we should wear modern fibre thermal tops but I go for a cotton or wool thermal shirt rather than synthetic fibre ones. Over the top of this I tend to wear wool, either a tightly woven shirt or woollen thermals (see page 21), and

Lowa military boots.

over them, a windproof jacket or a heavier wool shirt: if you are in the open go for the windproof jacket, the shirt in woods.

In this environment waterproof clothing is important so take jacket and trousers in either Gore-tex fabric or Triple Point. Don't forget a hat; try to find one that is insulative, windproof and waterproof.

Arctic

In the Arctic we are dressing against dry cold although on rare occasions it rains so protection from moisture is also important. Footwear must be chosen to suit the activity you are to be engaged in: for cross-country skiing choose the appropriate cross-country ski boots, two sizes larger than normal to accommodate felt inner boots for extra insulation and plenty of room. If your footwear – in fact any of your clothing in the Arctic – is tight it will restrict your circulation and you will get cold. Extra room is necessary.

If you are going to be working with snowmobiles and skis, instead of a conventional cross-country ski boot consider taking a rubber boot adapted for cross-country skiers, such as those made by Nokia. They give good protection from the moisture commonly encountered on a snowmobile when travelling over frozen lakes with a heavy snow pack on top. These boots also come with a felt inner liner.

In cold dry conditions when I am using snow-shoes, my favourite boots are mukluks, made from moose hide with a felt inner sole and plenty of room for the foot to move. The best are made by a company called Steger Mukluks. Inside them, I wear wool socks, a thin pair and a medium-thick pair relying for warmth on the felt liner.

I normally use wool underwear in the Arctic and my middle layers are wool: I take two pairs of wool long johns in different weights of wool density, and three woollen shirts, which can be worn over each other

again in three different weights of wool. Here I prefer Ullfrote fabrics, which are, without a doubt, the best for this environment; they come in 200g/m² to 400g/m² or 600g/m² weights, which makes it possible to create a perfectly balanced layered clothing system. The manufacturers claim that as the wool is of the highest quality it can be worn next to the skin without causing itching.

Headgear is very important in the Arctic, and worn for most of the time. Here I like a hat that combines rabbit fur with fabric. When the temperature drops I add either a wool skull-cap made by Ullfrote or, when I am travelling on a snowmobile, a full woollen balaclava.

I use two types of glove: British Army leather gloves with a Gore-tex liner are excellent for carrying out small, fiddly tasks in the cold; for using an axe, I wear woollen mittens produced in Lapland by the Sami people, called lovikka, with a leather Chopper mitt on top.

For emergencies, I also carry warm, windproof over-trousers and a down jacket for travelling in very cold conditions on snowmobiles or when I have to stand still for

Top: Rubber boots with felt inners adapted for skiers.

Bottom: Steger Mukluks for cold dry conditions.

200gm/m² 400gm/m² 600gm/m² Windshell

Ullfrote underwear in layers.

You can never have too many clothes when travelling by snowmobile. Wear goggles over hood so you can easily turn round and look behind.

In extreme cold an extra skull cap beneath your hat can make all the difference to warmth.

Lovikka mittens with leather over mitts.

any length of time. It is also useful to have thickly woven woollen trousers, some windproof over-trousers or ski trousers and a waterproof jacket. My own windproof outer layers are made of Ventile – a single-layer fabric trouser and a double-layer anorak with a fur hood. In the North artificial fur does not work as effectively as a real fur, and a fur ruff is vitally important when travelling on snowmobiles for any distance.

CUTTING
TOOLS

Four basic types of cutting tool are used in bushcraft:

- the knife,
- the saw,
- the axe,
- the parang or machete.

Each has applications to which they are uniquely suited. In addition, there are a few specialist tools for use in unique environments or to improve craft work and backcountry handicraft.

It is important to understand these tools: an inappropriately chosen cutting tool is inefficient and can be dangerous to the user. Also, cutting tools are heavy, so choose wisely rather than burdening yourself unnecessarily. Learn how to use each tool safely: this will take time, humility and careful practice.

THE KNIFE

The knife is your number one tool, with which you can make almost anything you need, cut up food or craft beautiful objects.

Choosing

When I started teaching bushcraft, students struggled to acquire skills because their knives were blunt, too large or folding-blade designs. Experience taught that even locking folding-blade knives can collapse on a finger and that they do not encourage strong, confident cutting because they flex at the hinge. When choosing a knife, take into account the following:

Size: Do not choose a knife with a large blade: we do not want to hack, but to carve. This is best achieved with a blade 8–12cm long.

Handle: It should be well designed for easy grip: avoid finger notches as they make it difficult to vary your grasp comfortably. Find one that is a comfortable shape and size for you to hold. Never use a knife with a symmetrical grip: in poor light or when you are tired, you may mistake the edge for the blade back and cut yourself.

Blade shape: It should have an edge on only one side: double-edge blades are for fighting. A spear-shaped blade is ideal, enabling the blade to be inverted and used to peel bark and skin.

Avoid blades that are very round, where the belly rises to the tip, as the knife will tend to slip off the work-piece at the end of each cut. Avoid serrated blades: they hamper good carving; you will be learning to sharpen your knife to a razor's edge, serrations will provide no appreciable advantage. The blade tang should ideally be full tang, i.e. extending the full length of the handle at full handle width. This is the strongest arrangement, although shortened or narrowed tangs are acceptable if well made.

Avoid blades with this strong a curve.

Guard: A small guard just in front of the edge is useful but by no means essential as it can interfere with sharpening and carving.

Steel: Any good cutlery steel will do, either stainless or carbon, but it must be easily sharpened and not brittle. My personal preference is for high-carbon tool steel, which meets all these needs admirably; although prone to rust this is a minor drawback, easily avoided by keeping the blade dry and clean. If you are working predominantly in a salt-water environment, opt for stainless steel.

A knife is the most important survival tool. Frustrated at not being able to find the ideal knife for my work I ended up designing my own, which went into production in 1990.

1. Tang *part of blade which extends into grip* | 2. Guard | 3. Choil | 4. Back | 5. Belly | 6. Edge | 7. Point | 8. Grip | 9. Pommel

Edge shape: Generally the grind shape of the edge is chosen by the manufacturer for ease and cosmetic appeal. Having experimented with each type of grinding – hollow, convex, secondary bevel and flat bevel – I have found a fine flat bevel grind to be the most efficient for cutting wood: it provides a sharp edge that slices efficiently and cleanly. It is prone to damage if you touch bone when skinning a large animal, but this can be avoided by modifying your butchery technique.

Safety

Before you consider using your knife, think safety. Bear in mind that, once sharpened, your blade will be razor sharp.

Stow your knife in a strong sheath. If you are hiking in fairly civilised country it can be carried in your rucksack. However, when you venture into remote regions, attach it to your belt or hang it round your neck and shoulder on a strong cord.

When the knife is not in use, even for a few moments, it must be put back into its sheath, which should be kept clean: clean your knife if it is dirty before sheathing it.

An old rule of bushcraft is never to lend your knife: a damaged knife may result in a broken friendship. However, if you have to pass your knife do so as illustrated, overleaf.

There will be times when you need to stow your knife safely for a few moments – tucking it under your armpit is a good method, but be careful not to slice yourself on withdrawal. Keep the edge facing downwards.

Whenever you pick up your knife, pick up your first aid kit too.

Carve away from the outside of your body. A common error is to sit down and carve on a piece of wood between your legs. If the knife slips you may sever the femoral artery.

Train yourself always to keep your

supporting hand behind the back of the blade, not in line with the cut or where a slip might slice into you.

Cutting technique

Every piece of wood has a grain structure that determines its strength and performance in a range of tasks. The structure varies from species to species: one wood might be suited to a task that requires flexibility; another might be resistant to splitting. The grain structure will affect the ease or difficulty you will experience in carving the wood: in learning to understand its behaviour, you will become able to predict the wood's likely response to carving. Then you will carve more easily, the grain assisting you.

- Think of a piece of wood as a tightly compressed bundle of fibres laid parallel to each other.
- If you wish you can split the wood apart by forcing a blade or wedge down into it from the ends of the fibres.
- If you wish to cut through the fibres it will be most easily achieved by slicing at an angle so that the load of the cut is applied to one fibre at a time rather than the massed bundle.
- You can cut through the grain at 90° only when the bundle is thin and you can exert sufficient force.
- If you can stretch the fibres until they are taut, they are more easily cut – just as it is easier to cut a taut string than a slack one.
- When you wish to carve deeply into a piece of wood you may need to sever the fibres at the end of your intended cut to prevent them lifting and splitting ahead of the blade: such a 'stop cut' is a fundamental technique of wood carving and requires forethought and careful consideration of the grain.
- You can carve against the grain if you do so lightly with a strong slicing action.

If you have to pass your knife do so as shown above.

Grips

The Forehand Grip

This is the grip you will use most often: it provides strength and power as well as good control. Note that the thumb is not placed on the back of the blade. The cut is made with the strength of your arm and back. A safe follow-through is essential with this cut, be it clear space or a cutting block.

Forehand grip.

The Backhand Grip

This grip is rarely used, except for when cutting a taut cord being held by someone else. By turning the edge towards yourself you are taking control of the risk and ensuring that the blade does not slip through the work-piece to cut someone else. The cut is made with the arm.

Backhand grip.

The Chest-lever Grip or Side Grip

In this grip the blade is held with its edge towards your knuckle, enabling you to place your thumb on the face of the blade. The knife is held horizontally across your chest, edge facing outwards, thumb uppermost. The cut is effected with your arm and an intake of breath. In this way your chest acts as a pneumatic ram, generating tremendous force, enabling you to use your hand strength to control the angle of the cut.

Chestlever grip.

The Reinforced Grips

Useful for fine work, the cut is effected with the thumb of the hand holding the work-piece pressing on the back of the blade.

Reinforced grip 1.

Reinforced grip 2.

CUTS

Making a hook: Slice in two crossing cuts.

Chip out the wood from three quarters of the cross.

Deepen the beak of the hook formed.

Front view.

Side view.

Spear notch: The spear notch is an easy way to notch the end of a stick.

Perforating: Scribe a rectangular hole.

Chip out the wood on the first side.

Scribe lines from front side around the edge to rear side.

Using lines and estimation repeat hole making, until holes meet in the middle

Clean out hole and make neat.

Trimming: By cutting in the direction of branch growth, use power and follow through so that the cut ends beyond the branch to be trimmed

Breaking: Make a series of small cuts around the work piece to weaken it, then snap it in half.

Shaving: Using a straight arm.

Shaping: By pivoting around the thumb.

Pointing: Using 3 clean cuts.

Truncating: Using a wooden baton

Draw knife

How to sharpen a knife

To sharpen your knife you will need a set of abrasive stones ranging from coarse to fine. At home you can indulge yourself with a set of large bench stones, while in the field you will need a small lightweight alternative. Abrasive stones are manufactured from a wide range of materials. My preference is to use Japanese water stones which work fast and conveniently to give a razor edge. Use three grits 800 for coarse, 1200 for medium and 6000 for fine. In the field carry a combination 1200/6000 stone sawn in half.

To use these stones soak them in water before use. Only use the coarse stone if really necessary, when you have seriously blunted your knife or damaged it. Lay your knife on the stone and raise the back until the bevel of the blade lies flat on the stone and now push the blade away from you as if trying to cut a thin layer from the top of the stone. Do this eight times before turning the blade over and sharpening the opposite face towards you. Now make eight more strokes alternating the faces of the blade. As you do this a paste will form on the stone, do not wipe this away as it helps to speed up the process; keep the stone wet by splashing it with water throughout the process. Move on to a finer stone and repeat the process. The 6000 grit stone need not be soaked, just wetted; preferably create a slurry on the stone prior to use with a small nagura stone (these are specially made for the purpose and can be purchased with your stones).

After using the 6000 stone clean the blade, then strop it on the inside of a leather belt 50 times, alternating the blade face on each stroke. This will help to ensure a sharp and

(1) Eight strokes away.

(2) Eight strokes towards, the eight alternating

(3) Towards the blade tip you will need to lift the grip to accomodate the blade curvature.

(4) Strop.

(5) Ceramic sharpening rod.

(6) Sharpening in the field.

How to sharpen a knife

How to carve a spoon

① Split the billet.

② Look for a section which has a natural spoon-like kink.

③ Carve in the shoulders of the bowl and flatten the sides of the handle.

④ Point the tip of the bowl.

⑤ Flatten the underside of the bowl.

⑥ Shape the underside of the handle leaving thickness at narrow points and thinning at wide points.

⑦ Essentially the spoon is now blanked out, with clean top, bottom and side shaping. Complete the spoon by whittling these sides with your knife so that the spoon shapes blend naturally and with grace.

⑧ Lastly, hollow the bowl with a spoon gouge or crooked knife. Do not make the bowl too deep.

Hand carved spoons are both beautiful and functional, and bring memories of the place and company in which they were carved.

durable edge. To complete the process I run the blade very lightly down the finest ceramic sharpening rod to give the edge more bite. If you do not have a ceramic rod use the edge of a car window.

In the field, employ a simpler approach: wet the small field stone and sharpen each side with a slicing action with pressure on the slicing stroke only. Do one face, then the other, then alternate as usual. If possible strop the blade; if a leather belt is not available a smooth piece of wood can also be used.

THE SAW

Saws are efficient tools, enabling us to cut up wood with minimum wastage. They are safer to use than the axe, particularly in poor light or after dark, and can be entrusted to a beginner with only a few minutes' instruction. Saws also enable us to trim green wood neatly in a way that is less damaging to a tree.

The folding saw

The easiest saw to carry and use. It is the perfect companion to the small sheath knife. When choosing a folding saw, ensure that the blade locks securely in the open and closed positions.

To work efficiently a saw must cut a groove wider than the blade is thick. This is achieved in folding saws in one of two ways. The most common method is to have the blade hollow-ground behind the teeth: these

Bushcraft gadgets

Top left: Note the use of the hook notch.

Top right: An elegant way to suspend the lunch kettle.

Centre: For the fixed or overnight camp, a pothanger with many hook notches gives flexibility and allows the heat control necessary for cooking breads and other outdoor fare.

Bottom: Simple rustic pot hangers.

blades cut well but are apt to snap in use, either at the tip or just in front of the handle, which means that they are not suited to wilderness travel where a saw will inevitably encounter rough usage. The alternative is a blade with teeth set wider than the blade: these are usually produced by welding very hard teeth on to a strong spring steel blade, and this is by far the strongest arrangement: the teeth stay sharp longer and cut a wider range of materials. In many years of issuing Sandvik Laplander saws to students, I have never had a blade break.

The bow or swede saw

An essential tool of a base camp where wood fires are employed. The bow can be fashioned from either a bent green branch, a carved frame or collapsible wooden frame; the best ones are oval tubular steel designs. Avoid saws that narrow at the forward end and saws that are excessively long. Ensure that it is equipped with its own mask; when not in use, mask the blade and hang it out of harm's way.

Generally speaking, hand saws are the safest of all cutting tools and injuries occur most when transporting a saw without its mask, or

Blade intended for dead wood

Blade intended for green wood

when the blade jumps at the start of a cut on to the back of your supporting hand. Obviously the saw should only be carried with the blade masked; if this is not possible consider removing the blade and coiling it inside a billy-can.

Safe cutting

When you initiate a saw cut, do so with your supporting hand passed through the bow of the saw; this will prevent the blade jumping and cutting you. Once the cut is slightly deeper than the depth of the blade, remove your hand and continue sawing with the

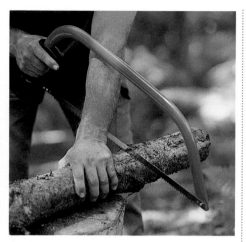
Start sawing like this to prevent the saw jumping out of the cut and on to the back of your hand.

Once established to a depth greater than the blade width, place your thumb over the cut.

thumb of your supporting hand pressed over the cut to lock the blade into it.

Support
Before cutting any wood with your saw make sure that it is well supported to prevent movement: this will ensure that the energy

you impart to the saw is fully transferred to the cut.

Although bow-saw blades are made narrow to reduce the likelihood of the blade binding in a cut that closes, this does happen frequently. To avoid it ensure that as the cut deepens, the wood is not supported in such a manner that the cut will close, gripping the blade. Not only is a trapped blade inconvenient, it will also be damaged: the kerf or set of the teeth will be narrowed. When felling a tree you can prevent the cut closing with a thin wedge driven in behind the saw blade.

Trimming a branch
When sawing down a heavy branch you must consider the force of tension within the limb. If you saw directly from the top surface of the branch the cut will open and eventually the branch will split free with unnecessary damage to the tree. Alternatively, if you cut upwards from underneath, you will avoid the problem of splitting but your saw will jam tight in the

Splitting wood

cut as it closes. Therefore cut a third of the way through the branch from the underside then cut down from above. By staggering the cuts we achieve a neat, stepped cut. With the main weight of the branch removed, you can now cut the branch cleanly near to the bole where it will heal correctly (see page 38).

Splitting

To split wood, take a section of relatively straight wood free of knots and saw half-way through it at the centre. Now with the cut upwards strike the log on a rock or fallen tree a third of the way beyond the cut. The top half of that end of the log should split off. Reverse the log and repeat the process with the opposite end. Finally snap or saw the long half of wood in two.

Cutting up firewood

If you have to cut up a long piece of dead timber into shorter more convenient lengths, do not waste energy laboriously sawing

through the wood. Instead cut half-way through it at intervals equal to your desired length of log. Then strike the log at these weak points on a nearby rock or log. Not only will you save energy, you will also extend the life of your saw.

Cutting green wood

When you cut green wood, do so only in a way that allows the tree to continue growing and remain healthy: for example, coppice broad-leaved saplings and remove only one branching tip from spruce boughs. If you need to remove a whole branch, cut it away cleanly with a saw at the bark scar where the branch joins the main stem. Done correctly the tree will heal itself, growing over to prevent infection by bacteria or fungi.

If you have to cut a sapling, do so in a place where there are several and choose one that is likely to be crowded by others. In this way you will be thinning the forest, allowing for healthier growth. Better still, look for a sucker from the base of a mature tree and cut it back close to the ground; several new shoots will spring from the old stump.

Fell a larger tree close to the ground in the tidy way of a professional forester.

THE AXE

There is a wide range of axe designs, from felling axes to axes for splitting and driving wedges. For wilderness travel your choice of axe will depend on the environment into which you are going. The further north that you travel, the more important the axe becomes.

With a well-set-up axe we can make things of practical value and things of beauty quickly, from wood that might otherwise only be burned. You can split firewood so that it will burn more efficiently or fit inside your stove. You can also remove fallen trees, which may impede your travel, and fell dead standing firewood in winter.

The drawback is that the axe is a tool that requires training and experience to master. It must never be handed to a novice without expert supervision. It should only be used in good light, and must be stowed away from harm in camp.

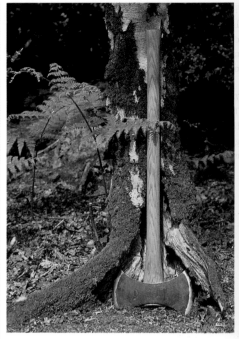

The way to safely stow an unmasked double bit axe in the crotch of tree buttresses.

Make of axe

For wilderness use you will need an axe that is made with passion by perfectionists: Gränsfors of Sweden.

1. Deer's Foot | 2. Knob | 3. Lanyard hole | 4. Helve or handle | 5. Belly of handle | 6. Grip | 7. Back (of handle) | 8. Head | 9. Cheek | 10. Lip | 11. Poll | 12. Eye | 13. Axe bit | 14. Edge | 15. Throat of handle | 16. Toe | 17. Heel | 18. Blade bevel | 19. Shoulder | 20. Wedge

Types of axe

In the wilderness you will need an axe that can perform many tasks and which can be used in one hand as readily as two. Several options present themselves.

The Wildlife Hatchet/Scout Axe

This is the axe most commonly employed by beginners: it is the lightest axe at around 750 grams – heavy axes cause strain and tiredness in the inexperienced user, which can lead to

held one-handed in the middle, provide a counterbalance effect that dampens rebound.

So long as this axe is used with care, and not used to tackle jobs that require a heavier axe, it is a first rate tool and a good partner to the bow saw for providing a fixed camp with plenty of sound firewood.

The Small Forest Axe

The number one choice for bushcraft. It weighs only 1 kilogram and its helve is 50cm

Forest axes: 1. Double bit working axe | 2. American felling axe | 3. Scandinavian forest axe* | 4. Small forest axe.* | 5. Wildlife hatchet/scout axe.* | 6. Pocket axe

*most useful for wilderness travel.

accidents. With a length of 36cm it is easily portable but can only be used one-handed and is effective for chopping firewood, or light axe carving, provided it is sharp. Some words of caution: the short length of the helve means that the Scout axe has little counterbalance action when it is used with one hand: if you strike a springy branch the axe may bounce back towards you. Axes with a longer helve,

long, so it can be used efficiently with one hand or pressed to bigger jobs with two.

The Scandinavian Forest Axe

A full sized two-handed axe, weighing 1.5 kilograms with a helve 64cm long. An experienced axe user will have sufficient strength to use it one-handed. I reserve this axe for use almost exclusively in boreal forest

Crafting axes: 7. Splitting wedge (only hammer with maul or splitting maul). | 8. Swedish broad axe | 9. Carpenter's axe | 10. Swedish carving axe | 11. Hunter's axe

in winter where the demands of limbing (removing) snow-covered branches, and chopping into the tight grain of slow-growing timber present tough work.

Caring for your axe

- Prevent the head rusting by keeping it dry; in bad weather rub it over with the end of a wax candle.
- Occasionally apply boiled linseed oil to the helve.
- Never lend your axe to a novice.
- Do not leave your axe stuck into a log for any prolonged time or it will become blunt.
- Never hammer one axe against another, and never use your axe with or against anything harder than wood.
- Try to avoid cutting into the ground as you may strike a stone that will damage the edge.
- Never chop on to rock or wood with nails driven into it.
- When using your axe in sub-zero conditions warm it with your hand to body heat first to make the steel less brittle.

- If you nick the edge of the axe, flatten the edge and resharpen it to the correct angle again.
- Never grind an axe on a dry or high-speed grinding wheel as you will spoil the temper of the blade. Do not sharpen the edge too thin – this often happens with a file – and unless it is intended to be so, do not hollow-grind the edge: the axe should have a flattish convex edge.

Basic axe safety

- Whenever the axe is not in use it should be masked with a strong case. At moments of rest during use it should be placed in safety either by setting it into a cutting block, the end of a log, or between the buttresses of a tree. Do not leave your axe set into a log for a prolonged period as the chemicals in the wood will attack the steel, blunting the axe.
- Avoid using an axe with a loose head.
- Keep children and animals such as sled dogs away from the axe.
- Be careful when walking with an axe in

Caring for your axe

Use the edge of a bench stone for this. In the bush I have used a natural rock for this.

Remove nick.

Sharpen in normal way.

your hand: should you fall or trip, cast it away from your body. Always remain alert to the edge, the direction in which it is facing and the proximity of other people. While it is often recommended that the axe is carried cradled in the palm of your hand, in practice this is impractical: axes are most often carried grasped at the throat. As with any other cutting tool, when you carry an axe make certain you're also carrying a suitable first-aid kit.

- When you come to use the axe ensure before you begin work that your clothing will not impede the swing – scarves or cumbersome outdoor clothing and waterproofs may get in the way. Next,

Whenever the axe is not in use it should be masked with a strong case.

make certain there are no obstacles that may impede the swing: ideally you should be in a clear space large enough that you can reach out with the axe end so that it represents the radius of a circle within which there are no obstructions.

- Whenever you use an axe, it is imperative that you should have a safe follow-through: a block, log or the ground to act as a backstop to your cut so that should you miss the work-piece or the work-piece breaks unexpectedly the axe will not pass through and bury itself in any part of your body or anyone else's. Instead it should fall harmlessly on to the safe backstop. Do not cut into the roots or trunks of living trees as this will damage them.

- If you are tired, consider whether you should be using an axe at all. Perhaps the job can be more safely achieved with a saw, or left until you are less tired. In poor light, when standing on snow, or if you're new to the axe, do your chopping in a kneeling position. This will ensure that the ground acts as the safe backstop.
- When you use the axe one-handed, you risk chopping the hand that is supporting the work-piece. To prevent this, pay attention to the potential path that the blade of the axe will follow. When using an axe, we vary the angle, force and intensity of blows as demand requires. This means that the axe will swing from a variety of pivot points: at the wrist, the elbow, the shoulder or even the back. In good axe work, each blow of the axe is considered before it is made. In any swing of the axe, stay alert to the pivot point, as this will dictate the size of a sphere of danger, which has at its circumference the furthest tip or toe of the axe blade. It is absolutely imperative that any body part within this sphere has either a block between it and the axe blade, or is behind the axe while cutting.
- Allow the weight of the axe head to do the work. In good axe work the axe head is simply lifted and dropped on to the work-piece with arm strength used only to guide it accurately rather than to force it down. If the axe is not cutting, you are either placing the blows badly or it is blunt.

How to free a stuck axe

If your axe becomes stuck in the chopping block you can free it by a sharp, downward blow to the tip of the helve. Failing this, use gentle sharp tugs alternating between up and down until it works free. Never apply sideways force to the helve or excessive force up or down: if you do so you will inevitably snap the handle.

Felling

In bushcraft we do not fell trees very often; usually we work with already fallen dead timber. However, in boreal forests it can be necessary to fell living trees, for tent or shelter poles, and dead standing timber, for firewood. Bear in mind that in the far north green birch is important firewood. In tropical rainforest it may be necessary to fell trees to create an opening in the forest canopy for helicopter rescue in emergencies.

In Siberia, the Evenk people use a heavy axe to fell small saplings with just two diagonally opposing chops at ground level, demonstrating 'maximum efficiency for minimum effort'. For larger trees, a more considered approach is necessary. However, before felling any tree, you must first study it carefully and look for any lean: it is easier to work with gravity than try to overcome it. Next, look for any dead branches trapped in the crown of the tree – the last thing you need is a dead branch landing on your head while you are chopping. Study the path that the falling tree will take, and try to avoid felling trees that will snag in standing trees.

Limbing and Trimming

Having dropped your tree, you will need to trim the branches. Start near the base of the tree and trim towards the top, always keeping the trunk between yourself and the limb you are cutting. Thick limbs may need preparatory cuts to speed their removal.

Chopping

Cutting the tree into useful sections is achieved by sawing or chopping and the former is more efficient. However, you may have no option but to chop. This is a

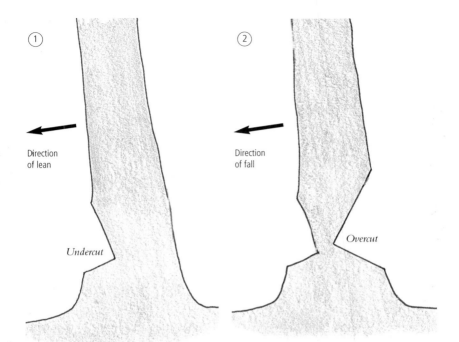

Felling with the axe alone

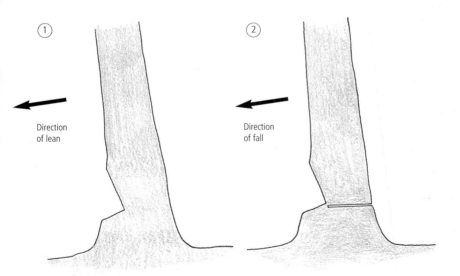

Felling with axe and saw

potentially hazardous activity. To chop through a log, you will need to cut out a V as wide at its opening as the log is thick. You will use an ambidextrous swing, changing your hand position to facilitate both left- and right-hand swings of the axe. Never attempt to bury the axe in the wood as it will stick. Instead, allow the axe to work at its own pace springing free nice-sized chips of wood. Once you have chopped two-thirds of the way through the log move round to chop from the opposite side and finish the job.

Common mistakes are to chop too hard and become tired, to make too narrow a V cut, and not to pay proper regard to the way in which the log is lying: it may be easier if repositioned.

Splitting

Perhaps the most common use of the axe in bushcraft. You must learn how to split a long piece of wood, and how to split short lengths for firewood. If you wish to split a tree into boards or splints for a specific purpose, you will need to cut wedges. Wedges made from wood are called gluts: they should be cut from

Place the axe on the wood to be split and bring both down simultaneously on to the block. This method is useful when a stump or flattened chopping block is not available.

strong wood types that will resist splitting when hammered. Never hammer a metal wedge with the back of your axe unless it is specially designed to do so: this damages the eye and loosens the head.

Splitting firewood on a chopping block is an essential axe skill. Ideally the block should be knee high, and the log to be chopped placed at the far side of the block to ensure a safe follow-through

If you do not have a chopping block you can

Note that the wood being split is placed on the far side of the block and when the axe passes through, it lands safely on the block. Ideally the block would be level and knee high; however, this is not always possible.

Reach up, out and around to ensure no obstructions.

1. Raise forward end of log slightly and measure up – aim to strike as shown.

2. Strike with a committed blow – concentrate on accuracy.

3. Strike with a follow-through.

improvise one by using the crotch of a forked branch or by a swift blow to the raised end of a knot-free, chopped or preferably sawn log.

Another method of splitting small logs or quartered logs is to place the axe on the log and bring both down on to a block at the same moment; this is a good technique for a beginner to use as there is a safe swing and

My favourite method of splitting without a block using the small felling axe. Note the raised-forward edge of the log.

follow-through. Make sure that the thumb of your supporting hand is not trapped between the axe helve and the log on splitting or you will bruise if not break it.

Flattering
To flatten a log, make a series of small chops an axe-blade length apart, then split out the wood between them.

Notching
Effort can be saved by weakening cuts to a long length of firewood, which can then be broken over a log or rock.

Hewing
Hewing is a technique to shape wood. You must cut down on to a block, and remember

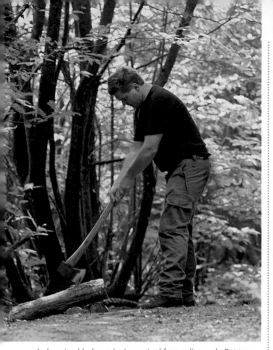

A chopping block can be improvised from split wood. But two pieces must be used to prevent the workpiece being spun upwards when struck.

Strike down on to the farthest log, bending your knees as the axe drops.

to keep your supporting hand out of harm's way: your fingers must stay on the opposite side of the work-piece to the axe blade and hew only below your supporting hand. If your hand tires, take a break.

Shaving

To shave feather sticks (see page 94) for kindling, grasp the axe head rather than the helve.

Slicing

Fine knife-work can be achieved by holding the axe head, with the helve upwards out of the way.

Fitting a new handle

Do not burn out the old handle, even if the edge is buried in damp soil: this will destroy the temper of your blade and ruin it. Instead, chip out the old helve, or drill it out at home

in your workshop.

Carve a replacement helve from seasoned wood, choosing hard wood such as hickory, ash, rowan or birch, depending on what is available. Carefully fit it to the eye of your axe, then split the top of the helve with your knife and a baton, and drive in a slender heart wood wedge – seasoned heart wood of oak is ideal. If you were able to salvage the metal staple that held the wedge in place, use this to further secure the new wedge.

A loose handle

If your helve becomes loose it will most likely need replacing. If you have just taken your axe to a drier, colder climate, however, you may find that allowing some linseed oil to soak into the eye rectifies the problem. In the bush, people often soak a loose axe head in water to make it swell and tighten. This is a short-term solution and the helve will eventually need

How to sharpen an axe

Sharpen your axe in a similar manner to your knife.

Eight strokes away, eight towards, eight alternate.

Strop on a leather belt.

In the field use a circular action on your cut down stone.

replacing. An extra wedge is another short-term measure but, again, it only postpones the inevitable repair.

THE PARANG OR MACHETE

The parang is the most dangerous cutting tool used in bushcraft. It has the longest edge, is used with a slashing action, which can be difficult to control, and is prone to deflection. For this reason we limit its use to tropical rainforest, or environments where similar materials need to be cut. Like all of the tools used in bushcraft, in the hands of an experienced craftsman the parang is fast and efficient. As with the axe, the secret is to allow the weight and speed of the blade to do the work.

There is perhaps more variety in quality in parangs than in any of the other cutting tools. When choosing a parang look for one that is not too long, 50–60cm is right for general-purpose use, with a stiff, heavy blade. Look also at the method by which the handle is attached: parangs commonly have a narrow

tang handle fitting, which may not be absolutely secure. Look for handles with riveted plate grips attached and a full, or nearly full, tang attachment. Once again, whenever you carry a parang, you must carry a first-aid kit. Keep your parang in a sheath or hard wooden case. When drawing it out ensure that you are holding the faces of the case and not the edge in case the blade cuts through the rivets or stitching and cuts your hand.

Never let anyone or anything distract you while you are cutting with a parang. If you are

A parang must be strong and sharp to chop tropical hardwoods and to trim materials like bamboo, here having been flattened out for flooring.

being bothered by an insect or are interrupted by a question, stop what you are doing until the disturbance has passed. Also, avoid getting into a cutting frenzy: considered blows are more effective. Also, assure yourself that you have a circle space around you the full length of your arm and blade within which to work.

Most of the work done with a parang requires a wrist action. It is important for efficient cutting that there is a clean follow-through, or space beyond the work-piece so that you can cut it and follow straight through beyond it. The best cuts made with a parang are done with a smooth, confident, swift action.

In pointing stakes a good parang will sever the pole at an angle of 30 degrees on the cutting block. It must be kept sharp, although chips in the blade are almost inevitable due to the rough and ready nature of the work to which it will be put.

As you make a cut ensure that no part of your body is in line with the parang's cutting edge and that other members of your party keep clear when parangs are in use.

Why carry such a dangerous tool at all? Neither an axe – nor a saw – is as versatile as the parang, which can be used to fell poles, create clearings, and trim away lawyer vine, which will snag your clothing. The parang will also open up access to a wide array of tropical foodstuffs from coconuts to heart of palm.

THE MULTI-TOOL

It has been said that a multi-tool is simply a collection of second rate tools, but its popularity speaks for itself. When we travel on off-road vehicles, snowmobiles, boats, motorbikes, or in helicopters we should of course ensure that we take a suitable tool-kit to effect repairs, but it always pays to have a multi-tool, equipped with needle-nose pliers and screw-drivers. Leatherman make a good one.

The multi-tool

SPECIAL TOOLS OF BUSHCRAFT

The crooked knife functions as a one-handed drawknife-cum-gouge. In north-eastern America it was much used by the first nations of that region to fashion everything from canoe paddles to snowshoes.

A smaller, more specialist version is the spoon knife, which enables us to hollow out a bowl or the bowl of a spoon.

Crooked knife and spoon knife

Digging tools

Occasionally you may need to dig a hole or excavate a root, and on the trail you can improvise a digging stick. In camp or if you are travelling by vehicle the best shovel is the Swedish Army entrenching tool: solidly made of steel it is virtually indestructible. It can also be fitted with an attachment for digging snow.

The digging stick should be fashioned

from hard wood with a tight grain. Find a log with a metre-long straight section, about 30–40mm in diameter, then carve one end either into a long, slender point for sandy conditions or into a chisel shape for hard clay. It can be made more durable by hardening the tip in the embers of a fire: scorch the wood slowly until it is about to turn brown and no further.

Black Diamond snow shovel: with an angled cutting edge it performs superbly in soft or hard snow.

confined space, when excavating a snow hole for example, but you will need a longer handle to dig a casualty out of an avalanche slide.

Avoid a round ball-grip handle on a shovel – it may be difficult to manoeuvre when your gloves are icy, particularly when digging out a snow cave or quinze. T- and L-grip handles suit mountaineers, who will probably be wearing gloves, but the best overall grip is the traditional D handle, which can be gripped easily by a mittened hand.

The snow saw

Useful in the mountains in winter as it will move snow quickly. It is an undervalued tool and not always easy to find. I prefer a solid, non-folding design, which, although bulkier, is stronger and more versatile than the folding kind. Failing this, you can use a small

Swedish army entrenching tool.

SNOW TOOLS

The snow shovel

Perhaps the most important snow tool. First decide on your main requirements: if you are a mountaineer, you will look for lightweight compactness; if travelling in the Arctic, you will need it to shift soft powdery snow; in either case, your snow shovel should be portable. Look for telescopic aluminium handles: they are strong and versatile. A short-handled shovel may be easier to use in a

Snow saw.

carpenter's saw which also provides the possibility of sawing wood for a shelter. Ensure that it is equipped with a mask.

The snow probe

A vital tool in avalanche areas. You should also wear avalanche transceivers to help rescuers locate you. A collapsible snow probe allows you to test the depth of snow and its hardness so that you can find a suitable place to construct a snow cave or trench. In an avalanche the snow probe will enable you to pinpoint a buried member of your party.

Snow probe.

WATER

Water is almost as important to humans as air, and in arid lands you must secure a source for yourself each day. This will dominate your route planning as your tracks join the blue dots on the map and you hope that each source will not have dried up. Never begrudge the weight of water in your rucksack: you must carry enough to last you on the way back to your previous source if the one ahead has vanished. Familiarise yourself with as many ways of finding water as you can until they are second nature, and ensure that you know how to make water safe.

Namib desert: the trees in the ravine show the presence of water even during the dry season.

THE IMPORTANCE OF WATER

In a temperate environment humans require between 3 and 5 litres of water per day, depending on clothing and level of exertion, rising to 10 litres or more in hotter climates. Water enables us to keep warm in cold weather and cool in heat. It aids digestion and transports oxygen and energy to the muscles and eliminates waste. When we are correctly hydrated, we should produce approximately a litre of light straw-coloured urine per day.

Dehydration

The effects of water loss are felt relatively quickly. Even under normal wilderness circumstances we can become dehydrated when water is available by failing to drink enough. Surprisingly dehydration happens more frequently in a colder environment than in a hot one. Arctic conditions sap the body of

moisture because the air is dry and the body needs more water to keep warm. Learn to recognise the symptoms of dehydration, and remember that it is easier to stay hydrated than to try to correct the effects of dehydration.

Symptoms of dehydration

The first and most obvious is thirst. Then you will experience discomfort that has been likened to the onset of flu, which may be accompanied by muscular aches and pains. Nausea sets in when you exert yourself and vomiting increases water loss. The nervous system is affected, leading to light-headedness or dizziness. Headaches, similar to a hangover, and tingling in the limbs are common, with irritability and reduced ability to make good decisions. Saliva and urine output is greatly reduced and the lips crack. The urine becomes darker. Gradually you will become disoriented, hearing may be reduced, and you may experience serious cramps and joint stiffness. Eyesight fails, coma ensues, then death.

People who live and work in hot climates are frequently in a state of minor dehydration, the clearest sign of which is infrequent urination and dark urine. While this may go unnoticed for long periods, the ultimate consequence may be kidney stones.

Preventing dehydration
In theory it is easy to prevent dehydration by drinking plenty of water, but in practice it is not always easy to achieve. Many beverages, such as tea and coffee, are diuretic, which reduces their benefit as a source of water. In extreme heat you may have to make a conscious decision to keep drinking, which is made difficult by the time and effort required to find and purify your water.

I ensure that I always carry sufficient water with me and a reliable means of purifying it. Each morning before the start of the day's activity I drink as much as I can, which makes it easy to maintain hydration throughout the rest of the day. Experience has shown me that it is easier to drink from a mug than a bottle, and if possible, I take with me a fruit flavouring for the water and use it well diluted. As the day progresses I drink frequently, and if an opportunity presents itself to refill my water bottles I take it.

FINDING WATER
Water Sources
Water sources are many and varied: some, like rivers and streams, are easily recognisable while others are all but invisible. To be proficient water collectors, we need to know how to locate sources, how to access them and how to

use them. We need also to keep an open mind: some of the most important water sources are the most off-putting to use. To locate water we must be able to track it across a landscape and understand its elusive nature.

From the moment a snowflake settles on a mountain top it begins a relentless journey down towards the sea. Water seeks the path of least resistance, seeping through cracks in the earth until it meets a layer of bedrock where it is forced by water behind to make its way upwards to the surface at a spring. As it flows across the land it gathers greater volume: the spring becomes a stream, then a

Indicators of Water

VEGETATION INDICATING WATER
- reeds
- palms, particularly the fan and doum palms
- willows
- alders
- ground ferns such as hart's-tongue
- figs
- casuarina trees
- wild sugar cane
- reedmace

INSECTS THAT INDICATE WATER
- bees
- wasps

ANIMALS DEPENDENT ON WATER HOLES
- wildebeest
- elephants - drink 100 litres at once and may go several days without drinking
- baboons
- monkeys – unreliable when edible fruits are available
- impala
- waterbuck
- bushbuck
- buffalo
- warthog

- hippo
- bush pig
- roan antelope
- red lechwe
- sitatunga
- burchells zebra
- mountain zebra – can go for up to three days without, and have been known to dig for water
- rhino – a less reliable indicator
- lion – a less reliable indicator, as they have been seen obtaining water from tsama melons
- leopard – a less reliable indicator
- kangaroo – will sometimes dig for water

ANIMALS THAT ARE NOT DEPENDENT ON WATER HOLES
- eland
- giraffe
- kudu
- red hartebeest
- gemsbok
- steenbok

BIRDS THAT INDICATE WATER
- finches – sometimes found at water holes or bore-holes in thousands, visible and audible from a distance
- pigeons and doves – drink mainly in the early morning and early evening
- grouse, particularly sand grouse
- guinea fowl
- herons

IN EXTREMES
In really desperate circumstances people have shot larger herbivores, for example elephants, and drunk the liquid from the stomach. To do this collect the foul-looking green mass from the stomach, wrap it in a cloth and express the moisture by wringing it tightly. The disgusting liquid that results is drinkable but should be left to clarify first. You can speed up this process with the addition of a small piece of liver. Only consume liquid from herbivorous animals; omnivores and carnivores may harbour harmful bacteria.

river and at last reaches an ocean.

Along its journey water gathers and discards pollutants, debris, viruses. Many potentially life-threatening waterborne pollutants are invisible to the naked eye, so we must endeavour to collect water from the most unpolluted source: the stream before the river, the spring before the stream. Good places to search for water are:

- the base of cliffs
- narrow canyons
- tight bends in dry river beds
- rock kettles (depressions in rocks) on sandstone outcrops
- places where differing geological formations meet, where animal trails to water holes converge, becoming busier and more distinct, often a clear indication of a water hole. Remain alert to signs that may indicate fouled water, such as dead animals.

COLLECTING WATER
Mopping
In an emergency dew is an abundant water source and we can emulate the desert beetles that specialise in collecting it. Early in the morning, take an item of absorbent clothing,

like a cotton T-shirt, and brush it across dew-covered vegetation. When it is saturated, wring out the moisture into a container. You'll be surprised by how easy it is to collect a large quantity of water. Be aware that while dew is perfectly clean the surface on which it condenses may not be. So, always sterilise water collected like this

A rock kettle in Namibia.

before you drink it. *Do not collect dew from the surface of toxic plants.*

Drinking straws
On its journey downhill water may become trapped in naturally occurring bowls such as hollow logs or sumps formed in impermeable rock. If you cannot access it by mopping, improvise a drinking straw from an available grass stalk or other non-poisonous hollow-stemmed shrub. Use your mouth as a pump to suck up the water, then feed it into a container. If possible, sterilise the water before drinking it. Avoid water trapped in the trunks of poisonous trees or tea-coloured water that has become badly stained by tannins leaching out of bark.

Improvised wells

Sometimes you may only be able to find pools of stagnant water or a patch of moist ground with no visible water. In these circumstances you can make a well.

Gypsy well

This technique is a way of obtaining water from saturated ground. Dug in saturated ground several metres from a stagnant pool, it

Dig into saturated ground.

Allow to fill with water.

Bail out first filling.

Second filling clearer.

can provide a way to obtain cleaner water than could be obtained from the pool itself.
1. Dig a round hole 60–80cm in diameter, until the bottom is 30cm below the depth at which you strike saturated ground. 2. Let it fill with water, which will be muddy. 3. and 4. Bail it out without disturbing the sides of the hole, then let the hole fill again. The water will be cleaner, especially if it is allowed to settle.

Frequently, this water is safe to drink as it is but if in doubt purify it. If you are intending to use the well for several days cover it with sticks or bark to prevent animals drinking from it and thereby contaminating the water.

On the coast a gypsy well can be dug behind sand dunes. Although most of the water that fills it will be brackish or salty, the topmost layer is rainwater or run-off, trapped behind the dunes. It is usually fresh, or fresh enough, for consumption.

Sip well

In arid lands water is sometimes trapped by rock under sandy ground, but digging will not release it. Excavate a hole to the diameter of a small fist in moist ground, and in the base place a small bundle of non-poisonous fibrous material, like grass leaves. Next put an improvised drinking straw – a strong grass stem with the node walls pierced through with a small stick – into the hole, resting it lightly on the bundle of grass. Now fill the hole, packing it tightly, but leaving the top end of the drinking straw exposed. Carefully pull the straw up about 1cm and begin to suck. You will eventually draw moisture from the soil into it, and, after considerable exertion on your part, water will gurgle to the top of the straw.

Fixed sip well

The fixed sip well is a cross between the sip well and the gypsy well, and is employed where it is possible to dig down into saturated ground. Dig a similar hole to that made for the sip well, fill the base with a grass filter and

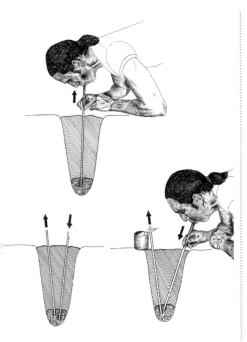

Sip well (above) and fixed sip well (below).

insert two drinking straws. Then back fill the hole. If you are confident that the water will be safe to drink, sip it through one straw – the other allows air into the hole to make the sucking easier. If you are in any doubt of the water's purity, blow into one of the straws,

which will force water up the other. Place a piece of bark or a broad leaf over the second straw to create a water fountain, which will run into a container. When not in use, the water straws can be plugged with small wooden pegs or twisted grass stoppers.

Reed well

Make a gypsy well (see page 60) and fill it with a bundle of reeds tightly bound with a withy. Cut off the bottom of the bundle and then cut out a bowl-shaped depression. The bundle helps to filter out soil from the water.

Rain traps

These may be fashioned from any large surface that can be arranged to feed the rain that lands on it into a suitable container. Avoid canvas tarpaulins or tent fly-sheets that have been treated against decay or may be tainted. A lightweight fly-sheet is ideal: if it is very strong it can even be used as the receptacle as it may be capable of holding several gallons. Large tropical leaves can be used as makeshift rain traps. Like dew, rainwater is safe to drink but it may be tainted by dirt from the collecting surface.

Dew traps

For water collection in the desert. Before sunset dig a pit 40–60cm deep and line it with an impermeable fabric such as polythene or a

Reed well

Dew trap.

Rain traps. These may be fashioned from any large surface that can be arranged to feed the rain that lands on it into a suitable container. Avoid canvas tarpaulins or tent fly-sheets that have been treated against decay or may be tainted.

lightweight fly-sheet. Fill this with large smooth stones, as clean as possible. Leave it overnight, and moisture will condense on the stones. Collect it before sunrise. Only small quantities of water can be collected from dew traps, and their performance will vary from season to season. Abandoned vehicles may also act as dew traps – again, try to exploit this resource before sunrise. Dew traps make good homes for scorpions so be careful when using them.

Water from vegetation

In emergency sufficient water may, perhaps, be obtained from your surrounding vegetation to take you on to the next reliable watering point. Here are some ideas.

A rack improvised from a split bamboo to collect water from many vines.

Vines

Many varieties of tropical vine, lianas and lawyer canes – such as *Ampelocissus martini, Entada phaseloides, Tetrastagma lanceoloria, Columella mollissima* – may contain liquid, but remember that plants suffer from drought just as we do. Chop out a 2-metre section of vine, making the first cut high up. As soon as you make the second cut low down, the capillary action holding water within the vine will

Water trapped in pitcher plants has been used as an emergency water source.

be broken and water will flow freely from the lowest end. You can slow it by holding the vine horizontally. Test the liquid for potability: it should be clear, not red, yellow or milky, and should not discolour when dripped into your palm. Next taste a drip: it should not cause a burning sensation in your mouth, or be bitter, or seem to dry your mouth. Vine liquid is

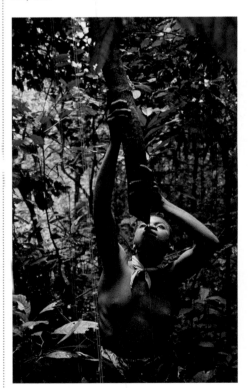

Completely at home in the jungle, this pygmy girl taught me my first lesson in the use of the water vine.

Top left: Large-sectioned bamboo sometimes holds water.

Top right: Fig trees can be tapped, giving many gallons. Water flows only at night. Do not allow toxic milky sap to contaminate the water.

Bottom right: A simple bamboo tube pushed into a banana plant gives a quick but limited supply of water.

Bottom left: Banana well – hollow out the base of a freshly felled banana plant, overnight this fills with water.

Opposite top to bottom:

1. Cut a 1m section from banana stem.
2. Peel off a layer and slice off a narrow strip to expose cells.
3. Fold along the removed strip.
4. Tilt to collect water.

refreshing with either no flavour or a mild, woody raw-potato taste. If only small vines are available you can make a rack to collect water from vines simultaneously.

Bamboo
Large-sectioned bamboo sometimes holds water, which can be located by tapping the stems with the back of a parang and listening for a lower tone and sloshing. Cut a small hole into the section to tap the water, which is usually safe to drink, cool and refreshing. Large quantities can usually be collected quickly.

Trees
Although not strictly a tree, a banana plant can be easily felled at about 30cm above the ground. Cut out the central portion of the stump, and the resulting depression will gradually fill with water. Let the depression fill completely before use: the first water is sweet and sticky, usually very rich in tannin, which may stain your hands blue-black. It may be a good idea to discard the first filling as the second will contain a lower concentration of tannin.

Birch trees can be tapped during the early spring, often yielding many gallons of sap, which can be used in an emergency as water but not in the long term. At other times of the year, this fluid can be obtained only by felling a tree so that the lower part of the trunk is higher than the crown. Chop through the top of the trunk, and fluid will gradually leak out. This is a drastic means of obtaining water, and it is unlikely that you will need to employ it, for where birch trees grow water is usually available. However, this technique has been employed with saplings in more arid parts of the world, including Australia.

Roots
Some desert plants store water underground in their roots. The Bushmen of the Kalahari dig up water-root, Kghoa, *Fockea angustifolia*, split open its leathery skin on one side with the tip

The leaf of desert kurrajong, an Australian source of water in arid lands.

of a digging stick, mash the pulp at the blunt end, then squeeze the juice into their mouths. The flesh can also be eaten raw after peeling. Other roots used by Bushmen include *Ipomoea verbascoides*, treated in the same way as Kghoa, and *Raphionacme burkei*, which is shaved finely with a sharp-edged stick then squeezed.

In central Australia the root of the desert kurrajong, *Brachychiton gregorii*, gives water. Examine the ground around the base of the tree for cracks radiating out from the tree, which indicate the location of a swollen root. It may be over a metre down, requiring considerable excavation. Once unearthed, peel off a short section of bark then shave it finely and squeeze it. Keep the remainder of the root, its bark intact, for future use. The swollen roots of young plants can be roasted and eaten after their bark has been removed, as can the large grubs sometimes found inside them.

In northern Australia the swollen root under a young red flowered kurrajong, *Brachychiton megaphyllus*, can also be used as a source of emergency water.

Top left. *Fockea angustifolia*.

Bottom left: *Raphionacme burkei*.

Top right: Scraped tuber flesh.

Bottom right: Squeeze flesh and drink liquid.

Red flowered kurrajong (*Brachychiton gregorii*) has distinctive seed pods.

Cacti

The barrel cactus is often mentioned as an emergency water source, but in fact only the fish-hook barrel cactus can be used: other varieties contain oxalic acid. Cut the top off the cactus, scoop out the pulp and squeeze it in a bandanna or other cloth until the liquid is released. Use these cacti only as a last resort: they make take hundreds of years to grow. DANGER: Do not confuse euphorbias with cacti. They look similar with their leathery exterior and spines, but unlike cacti, with their clear sap and bright emerald-green interior, euphorbias exude a white latex-like milky sap which is highly poisonous and will blister skin. People have died after eating meat cooked over a fire made with dead euphorbia stems.

Extracting water from desert kurrajong.

Fishook barrel cactus.

Top and above: The poisonous euphorbia.

Water by transpiration

Water is transpired from the leaves of plants. In arid areas where there is sufficient vegetation you can collect it in a clear polythene bag. Place the bag over a suitable leafy bough and tie it tightly to make an airtight seal. Sunlight on the leaves will cause condensation to form inside the bag, which pools at its lowest corner. If you constrict the corner of the bag, you will prevent the leaves soaking in the water and contaminating it by leaching of chemicals from the leaves. As this is a reliable technique, some armies issue transpiration bags as survival equipment.

Water from ice and snow
To eat snow or not
Don't melt snow in your mouth or hand: the amount of energy you lose will outweigh the benefit of the water gained.

Inuit iceberg technique
In the high Arctic the Inuit find an iceberg with a gently sloping surface of freshwater ice – identifiable by its deep blue colour and willingness to shatter. They scoop out a small bowl-shaped depression at the top of the slope, then prop over it a block of freshwater ice. Below the depression, they create a cascade of similar depressions, connected together with a finger-wide channel that they fill with soft snow. They light a fire with seal blubber and sticks cut from a sled board. As the fire melts the ice block, the water trickles under the seal-blubber fire and down through the cascade of depressions. At first the water is stained by fat and soot but is gradually filtered by the snow in the channel between the depressions. The water collects in a depression free from pollutants for drinking.

Finnish marshmallow
In Arctic conditions, cut a block of snow, push a large 'marshmallow' of it on to a stick, and hold it over a container placed to the side of a fire. The warm air slowly melts the 'marshmallow', generating a trickle of water.

Water-generating bag
When snow is too cold to make snowballs improvise a sack from an item of clothing or a

Left: The Inuit iceberg technique.
Top right: Finnish marshmallow
Bottom right: Water-generating bag

mosquito headnet, fill it with snow and suspend it to melt over a container placed beside a fire.

Melting in a billy-can

If you have a metal cooking pot do not pack it tight with snow. Snow is a good insulator; many a billy-can has been ruined by the fire working against the metal rather than melting the snow. Instead tilt the pot slightly on its side and heat it only gently as you melt very small quantities in the bottom, making certain that any steam produced can escape and will not become trapped by tightly packed snow. Be patient, adding snow until you have a depth of water into which snow can be gradually added.

The solar still

One of the most frequently described emergency means of obtaining water. Dig a sloping, rounded trench in saturated soil, place a container at the lower end, then drape over the entire trench a clear polythene sheet. Seal it around the edges and weight it in the

middle. Moisture will condense on the underside of the polythene and run down it to drip into a container. Note: although this technique works it rarely provides sufficient water to sustain life, and is only useful on sun-baked shorelines in super-saturated soil, or in riverbeds of arid lands where flash floods occur and the river sand is saturated.

MAKING WATER SAFE TO DRINK
Water purification

There are five basic contaminants: turbidity, parasitic worms, bacteria, viruses, and chemicals. Unfortunately no single method of water treatment will provide satisfactory treatment for all of these contaminants. So a combination of two or more should be employed. First, get to know the enemy.

Turbidity: this is dirty water which contains minerals, or particulate and organic matter that may make it cloudy or muddy.

To reduce the turbidity, look for the clearest water source and try to collect it from where it runs over rocks and is well oxygenated. If this is not possible, filter it by passing it through finely woven cloth, clean sand or, best of all, activated charcoal.

Parasitic worms and protozoa: these include embryonic roundworms, tapeworms, and protozoa such as amoebae (dysentery) and *Giardia lamblia* (beaver fever). Some of these organisms are relatively large and can be eliminated with a mechanical filtration device, or boiling. Chemical treatments are also effective if allowed sufficient time to work. However, cryptosporidium, which can cause life-threatening illness among the elderly, the very young and the sick, is resistant to iodine and chlorine and so brings into question the value of chemical-only water treatments. Fortunately it can be removed easily by filtration or boiling.

Bacteria: some of the most lethal water contaminants, they may be responsible for diarrhoea, dysentery, campylobacteriosis and E-coli. Because of their small size it is impractical to remove them by filtration but they can be destroyed by boiling or chemicals.

Viruses: the smallest health threatening micro-organisms, they can cause diseases such as hepatitis A & E and polio. They are destroyed by boiling or chemical disinfection.

Chemicals: pesticides, herbicides, fertilisers and heavy metals run off agricultural land, but are usually extremely diluted. Heavy metals are difficult to remove, but chemicals can be greatly reduced by passing the water through a carbon filter.

A strategy for water purification

Whatever purification methods we employ, our system must
- be effective at neutralising all the prime health threats
- be quick and easy to use
- be conveniently portable.

Filtration

Muddy water: in circumstances where clear running water cannot be found we may have to resort to muddy puddles. Pour it through tightly woven cloth, perhaps improvised from clothing. This can be made more effective by filling the filter with layers of sand and charcoal. Charcoal particularly will help to reduce off-putting odours and taste. The British Army have used a cloth filter bag, the 'Millbank Bag', for many years to remove mud from water. This lightweight reusable item of equipment can be carried as a standard item of your outfit. After filtering, sterilise the water before drinking.

Clear water: micro-organisms can be neutralised by boiling – usually the preferred option. Otherwise micro-filter it through either a ceramic or an activated carbon filter to remove parasites and some larger bacteria. Then treat the water chemically to ensure neutralisation of smaller bacteria and viruses.

Chemical treatment of clear water alone can prove effective but is less reliable than when employed in conjunction with micro-filtration.

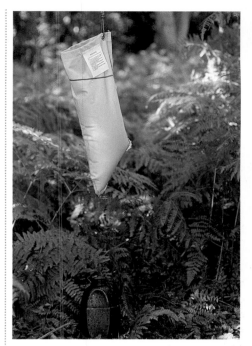
The 'Millbank Bag'.

NOTE: When purchasing a pump-action water-treatment device, be sure to establish whether it is a filter or a purifier. Purifiers filter the water and chemically disinfect it, killing all parasites, protozoa, bacteria and viruses. Filters alone cannot remove viruses and rely on a second stage of purification, either boiling or chemical disinfection.

Boiling

Boiling is a reliable method of sterilising water. Simply bringing water to the boil is sufficient to kill viruses, bacteria and parasitic cysts, even allowing for the lower temperature at which water boils at high altitude. It is necessary only to bring the water to the point at which the water is bubbling furiously. A cooking pot fitted with a lid will boil faster than without, and will use less fuel. Also, less water is lost as steam.

In regions where you are concerned about chemical pollution, empty the kettle before you fill it to prevent build up of a more concentrated solution.

Chemical disinfection

There are only two chemicals in wide usage for water purification: iodine and chlorine. The difficulty in using either of these chemicals is in achieving an accurate dosage: the aim is to destroy micro-organisms but add the least possible disinfectant. Use the forms of these chemicals that are specifically intended for water purification and ensure that you follow the manufacturer's instructions.

Bear in mind that temperature affects the speed with which chemicals destroy micro-organisms. Both chlorine and iodine act more slowly in cold water so you must increase the length of time in which the chemical has to sterilise the water before use.

Turbid water may shield micro-organisms from the disinfectant: in cloudy or discoloured water increase the chemical dosage to effect a certain kill. Most manufacturers provide guidelines on the bottle or packet for dealing with this eventuality.

Chlorine

Most usually administered as either tablets or droplets. It is an effective treatment, but moderately alkaline water in chalky/limestone regions inhibits its ability to destroy micro-organisms so contact time must be increased. It is not suitable for use without filtration in water that contains organic detritus. Also, it generally requires a longer contact time than iodine, which may be a significant drawback in extreme conditions. It can be used safely by those who may have an allergy to iodine or a thyroid complaint.

Iodine

Usually administered as droplets, tablets or by passing the water through iodine resin beads.

It should be avoided by people with thyroid complaints, an allergy to iodine, or pregnant women. Generally iodine has fewer drawbacks than chlorine: it remains active in alkaline water, is less affected by organic matter and is faster-acting.

Employing chemical purification

As always aim to find the cleanest water you can. If it is very muddy, clean it first by passing it through a filter, as described on page 71.

The water can be treated in one of three ways:

1. Directly with either iodine or chlorine drops or tablets. Use a strong enough dose and make sure that the contact time is long enough to treat protozoa like cryptosporidium, which is more resistant to chemical purification. Water treated in this way develops an unpleasant taste.

2. Pass it through a micro filter such as a ceramic filter, then treat with either iodine or chlorine drops or tablets to kill smaller bacteria and viruses. This is more reliable than 1 (*above*) as the water has been cleaned of parasitic cysts, which may be resistant to chemicals, and larger bacteria prior to disinfection. More time-consuming, it is a reliable method.

3. Pass it through a purifier that combines filtration with iodine-resin bead disinfection. This ensures that the water is both filtered and purified in one operation. Also, the iodine dose is more accurately controlled; the negative charged iodine molecules are attracted to the positive charged micro-organisms as they pass by.

Right: Pumping river water through a purifier in the rainforest, Mosquito Coast, Honduras – a daily chore worth the effort.

There are two varieties of purifier:

- Those that leave a residual presence of iodine in the water. It is detectable by taste but not unpleasantly so, and ensures that the water does not become reinfected after leaving the purifier, for example by decanting it into a dirty cup or water canteen. It is also an excellent wound wash.

- Those that remove the iodine as the purified water leaves the device, a good choice for people who are unable to consume iodine. In use, the operator must be scrupulous about keeping the exit port free of contaminated water (not always easy) and ensure that the water canteen or other receptacle is kept clean.

Improving the taste of chemically treated water

Both chlorine and iodine impart a strong flavour to water. This can be rectified by three processes:

- neutralising the chemical with another, such as sodium thiosulfate or ascorbic acid (vitamin C)
- removing the chemical after purification by passing the water through a carbon filter
- leaving the water in a clear canteen in strong sunlight.

While these processes improve the flavour of the water, they also halt any anti–microbial action.

SEA WATER AND BRACKISH WATER

There are only two practicable solutions for the removal of salt from water: one, to distil the water, or two, to use a reverse-osmosis pump to remove the salt mechanically.

Distillation

This can be difficult in the wilderness, and you will need suitable materials to improvise a still. Take a jerry-can and fit a pipe either to its opening or, better still, to its spout and attach it to a piercing in the can. The pipe is then fed either through a cooling tank of salt water into a receptacle or into a suspended plastic bag where steam can condense. The jerry-can is filled with salt water to about half its capacity and heat is applied beneath it from a fire or stove. You will have to distil a huge volume of water to produce a relatively small quantity of drinking water.

Reverse osmosis pumps are expensive, slow to operate and prone to mechanical failure, which places them beyond practical use except at sea.

FIRE

There are many ways to light a fire, from using the obvious tools, like matches, to improvising with some unlikely raw materials. As with all bushcraft, the secret to consistent success is to be found in the detail. Take nothing for granted.

PRODUCING A FLAME
Matches

Introduced in 1827, the friction match is simple to use and has no mechanical components to fail, so it is not surprising that it remains the most popular means of producing a flame. In our daily lives we strike matches without a second thought, and in the wilderness, too, they are a reliable means of firestarting, even in the worst weather. But matches must be treated as a finite resource and protected from their worst enemy: moisture.

There are several types of match available, and the quality varies enormously. In some countries they are made from woods that do not ignite very easily, so it is a good idea to experiment before making a choice. Check that the head burns smoothly and the stick catches light easily.

Strike-anywhere matches

These old-fashioned matches are my first choice for wilderness travel. Nowadays for safety reasons they are less popular for everyday use – if they are bounced about

over-enthusiastically or exposed to a sudden shock that generates friction between the heads they have been known to catch light. In the wilderness, however, their versatility is an advantage; they can be struck against any rough surface, from a zip to a rock. They are also the easiest type to look after as only the matches themselves, and not the box bearing the striking surface, must be kept dry.

Safety matches

Basic safety matches: These are the most common matches, the kind that need to be struck against the special surface on the side of the box to produce a flame. Both the matches and the striking surface must be be protected against moisture.

Water- and wind-proof matches.

Waterproof matches: The heads of waterproof matches have a coating of lacquer that guards against moisture damage. However, the striking surface must still be protected. Also it tends to wear out quickly because the layer of lacquer on the match heads makes them harder.

Stormproof matches: Stormproof matches are prey to the same complications as the waterproof variety. However, the stormproof match continues to burn even in windy conditions. The problem is that it may not produce a flame until the head has finished burning, by which time the matchstick has become very short.

Barbecue matches: These burn long and hot and can be an excellent emergency lighter. Some hikers use them as a convenient fuel for brewing a drink.

Barbeque matches.

Protecting your matches from moisture

Stow your match supply in several waterproof containers distributed throughout your kit. If you must carry matches in your pocket ensure that the match surface is airtight to prevent your sweat dampening them. Remember

Making a matchbox from a used shotgun shell.

Take two used shotgun shells and heat the brass end of one until it can be pulled free of the plastic case. This becomes the cap. At the base of the second shell, saw in striking grooves. Trim away the folded end, wax slightly and fit cap.

never to touch them with wet hands. You can insulate matches against moisture by dipping their heads in lacquer or candlewax, which will also aid combustion. An old trick is to set them head to tail in wax in the matchbox. This is an excellent idea for an emergency supply, particularly on waterborne expeditions.

Drying matches

One ploy to restore damp match heads that sometimes works is to pass the match through your hair a couple of times.

Matches that have become totally soaked can sometimes be saved as long as the heads have not dissolved. Lay them carefully to dry in the sunlight or in the dry, warm air of a cabin (not beside a fire or stove, obviously). Or place them on a dry rucksack, tucking the sticks under a strap to stop them blowing away.

Striking a match correctly

Preparation is the key to all firelighting. Before striking a match ensure that you have to hand

Making a matchbox from birch bark.

- Cut a strip of bark as shown. Fit tabs through triangular holes.
- Carve wooden lid and fit with a leather or bark tab.
- Carve wooden base and inset a piece of bone, grooved to act as a striker.

Striking a match correctly.

a mass of dry kindling and a candle or another means of extending the life of the flame.

Hold the match between your thumb and index finger, supporting the head against the striking surface with your middle finger. At an angle of 20 degrees sweep the match on to the surface so that the pressure is applied along the length of the stick. If you strike it at, say, 90 degrees, the side of the matchstick will absorb the force of the action and break. Once you have struck the match, remove the supporting finger to avoid burning it and cup the match in your hand against the wind, allowing the stick to ignite with a strong flame before transferring it to your tinder. Don't drop the matchbox: it might get lost or wet. Hold the match below your tinder so that the flame just licks into life. If you hold it too close the tinder is liable to extinguish the flame.

Leaving matches in cabins
All across the forested northlands there are

Northland etiquette demands that you leave the cabin as you would hope to find it.

cabins used by fishermen, hunters and trappers.

Leave the cabin as you would like to find it, complete with everything the next visitor will need. Ideally this should be a small stack of feather sticks, some split kindling and firewood. If the cabin is sound and dry, leave box of matches with the ends of the matchsticks protruding from it. This small courtesy has saved lives when travellers in difficulty have finally made it to a cabin with hands so severely frostbitten that it has been impossible for them to open a matchbox.

Lighters
If you are travelling in cold, wet weather carr a lighter with you, preferably the type that burns liquid butane gas, like a blowtorch, and has an integral cap to keep the working parts dry. If you can't get one with a cap, store you lighter in a small, dry bag or in a smoker's oilskin with some tinder.

Tinders and spills
Directly igniting kindling with your lighter will waste fuel. Instead put the flame of the lighter to some tinder, and use that to light th kindling.

Birch bark: Birch bark curls inwards on itself a it gets hot, making it both difficult to handle and inclined to snuff itself out. To prevent thi fold the bark like a paper fan to stiffen it, which will stop it curling.

Rubber tyre: When travelling in rainforests I carry my lighter in a smoker's oilskin along with some small strips of rubber, about 3 or 4cm by 1cm and 0.5cm thick, cut from an ol car tyre. This is a first-rate emergency firestarting outfit for anyone traversing wet terrain or involved in wilderness-based water activities. It resists all forms of moisture from sweat and general humidity to a thorough soaking when you are wading across deep

Birch bark spill, folded to prevent curling.

The NATO matchless fire-set.

rivers. When ignited these strips of rubber burn long and reliably, and two or three will create a good heart to your fire.

Camera film: In an emergency, ordinary camera film can be used as tinder. Tear off five or six 15cm lengths and fold each lengthways three times, concertina fashion. Holding them bunched together, light the ends and use them as a torch to ignite your kindling. Take care not to inhale the fumes they give off.

Magnesium block with artificial flint striker.

Sparks

Probably the most versatile of all firestarters are lighter flints made from a pyrophoric alloy. When scraped against a hard edge, these produce a shower of white-hot sparks. Spark-generators are available in a wide range of shapes and designs, from complex devices with the flint spring-loaded against an abrasive wheel to more simple versions activated with an edged tool. Some even come attached to a block of magnesium that can be scraped to produce shavings, which can then be ignited with the sparks.

Strike force artificial flint striker. Emergency tinder can be contained in the box section.

My preference is for a simple but thick, strong sparking stick, which you scrape hard to produce a shower of sparks. Not only does this device work the best, it lasts for years. It will even ignite chemical firestarters, such as wet-start firelighters, hexamine fuel tablets partially crushed into powder.

A simple artificial flint striker becomes a constant companion.

Scrape up a mass of fine bark shavings from a sheet of bark.

Place fire stick near to the shavings.

Use back of knife to shave sparks, pulling stick against blade.

Sparks falling on shavings will ignite the bark.

Its principal advantage is the almost endless variety of natural tinders it can ignite. Here are just a few examples:

- birch-bark peelings (peel only natural shedding bark)
- feather sticks of willow, spruce, and cedar, by dropping the spark under the last shaved curl
- all plant downs
- dry grasses
- shredded bark
- any fungi that can be used as tinder (see page 84)
- finely powdered oil-bearing shale
- tissue paper, teased thin
- candles with the wick teased out finely
- dry powdered herbivore dung
- red cedar bark scraped to a down

One of the most useful applications of the sparking stick is reigniting a burned 'fire dog' – a stick left with its ends partially burned after a fire has gone out. Strike the sparks on to the white ash-like area behind the charcoal end. When they take, blow on them to coax them into life and bring another ember alongside the new one to encourage it to grow larger. Once three sticks are aglow, fire should follow swiftly.

The main drawback to this kind of firestarter is, once again, its susceptibility to damp. This is less of a problem with the thicker sticks, and one that usually occurs when they are left in storage. On the trail they will be in daily use, which means that they won't be exposed to moisture for prolonged periods, but don't keep them in a damp pocket for any length of time.

Traditional flint and steels

The original flint-and-steel firestarter was made from iron pyrites and flint.

The technique used to create the sparks is easy, although it produces fewer and they are not as hot as those produced by other methods. Small sparks are struck from the iron pyrites with the edge of a flint blade on the tinder. Once a good spark lands on a fine fibre of tinder it catches and can be coaxed alight then transferred to a bundle of finely teased grass or other inflammable vegetable fibre and blown into flames.

If you want to try this method, assuming

Flint-and-steel.

'n the Neolithic period this was a typical fire set – flint blades, bone awl, freshwater mussel shell, nodule of iron pyrites, flint strikers, *fomes* tinder fungus.

Striking sparks into a mass of char cloth.

that you have access to a piece of flint. chert or similar hard, glassy rock, the difficulty will be in finding a suitable piece of steel: it must have a high carbon content and be tempered to the correct density. The steels used to make modern knife blades rarely give sparks, but some old-style carbon-steel knives have blades that do so, as will old metal files or the tops of some axe heads. If you can get hold of a piece of high-carbon steel you can make your own fire steel by heating the metal to a cherry-red colour and quenching it in water to around 40 degrees Centigrade.

Hunters can open shotgun shells to obtain tinder easily ignited with sparks.

Clematis (left), kapok (right).

Tinders for use with sparks

Tinders for use with a traditional flint and steel need to be very fine and to take a spark easily.

Plants: Some plants produce downy seed heads that can be used to take a spark. These include:

Cedar bark being shaved up for tinder.

- Rosebay willowherb: collect the downy seed-heads, clean them of the remains of the seed-head cases and scorch the edges to take fine sparks.
- Cotton grass: used by the Inuit.
- Poplar: soak the down and dry it under compression; the edges need to be charred for use with fine sparks
- Cat-tail: treat in the same way as poplar down
- Thistle: difficult to use with all but modern sparks

- Clematis down: also best used with modern sparks
- Kapok: tropical tinder used with sparks

Fungus: The trusty cramp ball, *Daldinia concentrica*, is such good tinder material that it can even be used in place of charcoal to cook over. It does need to be totally dry to ignite successfully. Choose a fungus that is very dark brown in colour and which, when broken open, reveals silvery-grey concentric rings. Strike the sparks on to these rings and the fungus will glow and smoulder. Blow gently on to it to increase the glow until the fungus is burning like a charcoal briquette. Cramp ball is common in the UK, but rare in the rest of the world.

The classic tinder fungus, the horse's hoof fungus *Fomes fomentarius*, can still be found growing on dead birch trees in northern latitudes or on dead beech in southern Europe. The fungi

Cramp ball fungus.

Horse's hoof fungus.

are best collected when they are young, when the apex of the hoof-shaped body can be easily depressed with the thumb. Slice off the horny outer surface (cuticle), and carve away the underside, which resembles thousands of tiny tubes (the pores). You are left with the trama, the leathery brown layer that can be used for tinder. Place the fungus on a smooth, wooden surface and immerse it in water, bring it to the boil and simmer it for twenty-four hours. Then gently pound it into a large, flat sheet using a wooden hammer. To improve the sparking quality either boil again for another twenty-four hours in a concentrated solution of hardwood ash and water, or rub hardwood ash into the fungus and massage it until it is dry.

Several other species of fungi can be prepared in the same way to produce tinder.

- true tinder fungus (*Phellinus igniarius*)
- artist's fungus (*Ganoderma applanatum*)
- *Ganoderma adspersum*
- maze-gill fungus (*Daedelia quercina*)
- blushing bracket (*Daedalopsis confragosa*)
- *Fomiotopsis pinicola*

Take some time to familiarise yourself with one of these types of fungi and investigate its trama layer. Then, should you find yourself in need of tinder in a strange land, you may be able to find a similar fungus that will do the job for you.

Char cloth: Char cloth is one of the most easily produced tinders for use with the flint-and-steel. It is simply cloth that has been burned until it turns very dark brown or black. Use a natural fabric, such as cotton, linen or silk. The quickest way to make it is to set light to a small piece of cloth then stamp the fire out when it has burned to the required colour. A more efficient method is to pack the cloth tightly into an airtight tin and pierce a small hole in it. Put the tin into a fire. As the cloth inside chars, you will see smoke escaping from the hole. When smoke is no longer produced remove the tin from the fire and seal the hole. After the tin has cooled you should have a container of perfectly charred cloth.

Wood punk: Dead, dry, soft decaying wood can sometimes be crumbled and used as spark tinder. Resinous wood punk, such as spruce, ignites well from sparks produced by modern sparking tools, while willow can be slightly charred to accept a spark from traditional flint-and-steel.

Fire by friction
Drill and Bow: Of all the friction techniques, the drill-and-bow method is the most efficient and reliable, even in the worst weather. It can also be used in any environment.

It involves drilling one piece of wood into another at 90 degrees to the grain. The drill is pressed against the hearth by means of a bearing block and is rotated by means of a string secured tightly in a bow, for single-handed operation, or fitted with toggles for a team effort. The advantage of this technique is that considerable force can be applied to the fire set in both rotation and downward pressure. This means that a greater variety of woods can be used than is the case with other friction methods, which in turn makes it more suitable for a wider range of conditions and environments. The material available for the string is a limiting factor. Strong cordage such as rawhide or nylon cord, being more resistant

Bearing Block

Drill

Bow

Cord

Hearth

Ember Notch

Ember Pan

to abrasion, can cope with many different kinds of wood, whereas plant-fibre cords, which are less resilient, reduce the choice of wood. The driest dead wood is ideal for this technique, but I have produced fire from green wood.

As with all bushcraft skills, it pays to practise this one before you need to depend on it. The key to successful bow-drill firestarting is choosing the correct wood for the drill and hearth. Early observers of friction firelighting maintained that the most important factor was having a drill harder than the hearth board. In the case of the hand drill this advice has some validity but with the bow drill it can be safely ignored.

True, some hard-soft combinations will work, but more often the harder wood consumes the softer variety without generating an ember, and when it does, the resultant erosion gives a shorter life span to the fire set. A more reliable principle is to select the same wood preferably from the same branch for both drill and hearth, using pieces as near as possible to the right size to minimise the amount of carving you need to do. This way the drill and hearth consume each other at a more even rate and you reduce the amount of experimentation necessary with unfamiliar wood. You will need wood that is dead, still standing and as dry as you can find. It should be only just possible to dent the surface of the wood with your thumbnail. In extremely wet weather you may have to whittle the drill and hearth from the dry centre of a large timber.

The crucial dimension of the bow-and-drill set is the drill diameter. This can vary from wood to wood. Generally smaller diameters suit harder woods and warmer climates, and larger diameters softer woods or colder, damper conditions. An average diameter of 25 to 30mm will work with the widest range of woods. Make the drill 220mm long and absolutely straight, carving the top to reduce friction and the bottom to maximise it. Then fashion the hearth board, ensuring that it is wide enough to comfortably accept your

Making a bow drill

If possible use a convenient crotch in the bow stick to secure one end of the cord.

Detail of bearing block showing depression; fill this with green leaves as a lubricant before drilling.

Top end of drill carved to minimise the friction surface.

At the thick end of the bow stick carve a depression to assist in securing the bow string in place.

Bottom end of drill carved to maximise the friction surface.

Drill into the hearth until you have seated the drill into a depression the same diameter as the drill.

Detail of the ember notch, a ⅛ segment removed from the hearth to allow friction dust to collect and form an ember.

The ember pan – bark, a shaving or a knife blade – is placed under the notch to collect the ember and protect it from the cold, damp ground.

The bow cord is wrapped around the drill so that the drill is on the outside of the bow.

drill. The bow should be 70cm long and inflexible. For the bearing block, use a wood harder than the one you choose for the drill and carve a small recess into it to accept the top of the drill. All you need for the ember pan is a shaving of wood or small piece of dry bark.

When you have all the components ready, make a slight depression in the hearth board to accept the drill. Drill down until the drill has seated itself in and has scorched its working end to its full diameter. Now carve away an eighth segment from the hearth. Fill the recess in the bearing block with green leaf material as lubricant.

When using the bow-and-drill, aim for stability. Pin the hearth firmly to the ground. Twisting the drill tightly into the bow cord, so that it is outside the bow, place its lower end into the hearth depression and hold it there by means of the bearing block. The bearing block must be securely anchored against your shinbone to prevent wobble. Drill smoothly and firmly, starting slowly and gradually increasing speed and pressure. When the hearth begins to smoke furiously, keep drilling for at least twenty more full strokes with the bow. Now gently lift the drill and bow out of the way. The notch in the hearth board should be full of a dark brown, smoking powder that clings tightly to the edge of the ember notch. Very carefully, position a small stick on top of the ember as you rotate the hearth away. The ember should be self-supporting and smoking. Fan it gently with your hand to encourage it to coalesce before lifting the ember pan and transferring it to a tinder bundle, where it can be blown into flames. The bundle must be tightly packed. A common mistake is to leave the fibres too open, which makes it difficult for the ember to grow. Place the ember into the finest part of the tinder and gently pinch it with the fibres, ensuring that you don't crush it. Holding the tinder 20cm from your face, blow softly into the bundle, watching for a

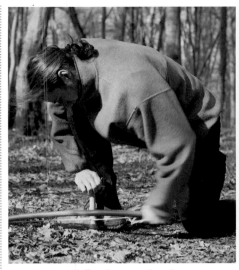

To use the bow drill efficiently you must have the correct posture and form to provide stability, and allow an easy drilling action with one arm whilst the other maintains a steady downward pressure.

glowing ember and developing smoke. Each time you take a breath, sweep the bundle away and down from your face, drawing it back up in time with your breaths. As the ember gradually spreads in the bundle the smoke increases. When it becomes thick and white, pause briefly to check that your kindling is ready to take the burning tinder. Just before the bundle bursts into flames the smoke will darken and turn greenish. When you see this happening, puff into the bundle to produce flames.

When you have got the hang of this technique experiment with other types of wood, or even try making a bow-and-drill in foreign climes. If you are working with unfamiliar woods, bear in mind that there are three main variables: the diameter of the drill, the speed with which the drill rotates and the amount of downward pressure you apply. Narrower drills tend to cause problems unless the wood is very hard or the conditions very dry. You are likely to achieve the best results if

you keep your drill as thick as your thumb at its knuckle.

BOW-DRILL	Elder	Marula
WOODS	Elm	Oak
	Fir (Balsam)	Pine
Alder	Hazel	Poplar
Aspen	Hibiscus	Wild rose
Baobab	Horse	Saguaro rib
Birch	chestnut	Sotol*
Cedar (red	Ivy*	Spruce
and yellow)	Juniper	Sycamore*
Cherry root	Lime*	Willow*
Clematis	Field maple	Yucca
Cottonwood	Norway	
Cypress	maple	*best woods

Drill and hand: The hand drill is the world's most widespread friction firestarting method. However, it has a limited range. In the north of the temperate zone, where the weather can be cold and is predominantly wet, it is less dependable.

Hand drills can be produced in the field, but are more often prepared before the traveller heads out on the trail. They can be made from a wide range of woods, including many shrubs that will not withstand the more vigorous action of the bow drill. To make a special hand drill set in advance, select a suitable wood, such as elder, with as little pith as possible. The base of secondary-growth elder sticks is thick-walled, as is the whole of a primary shoot. Shave off the bark, smooth the stick and straighten it gently while it dries. If you have a fire, use this to hasten the drying process.

If you need to make a drill on the trail look for dead, dry drill wood, for example white willow, mullein, teasel, dog-rose stem or even a dead, dry burdock stem. In aboriginal Arnhemland, a red-flowered kurrajong stem killed by a previous season's burn is ideal. The drill will need to be 50–70cm long and as straight as possible. Smooth the stick with a sharp edge so that it is as smooth as a dowel rod. Any bumps left on the stick are apt to produce blisters. If you cannot find a long,

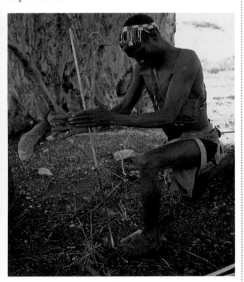

Hadza man in Tanzania using fire drill – note long drill.

Arnhemland, Australia – virtually identical technique.

HAND-DRILL WOODS	HEARTH WOODS
Alder	Alder
Aspen	Aspen
Baobab	Baobab
Bamboo	Blackboy
Blackboy	Burdock
Buddleia	Cedar
Burdock	Clematis
Cat-tail	Common
Common	corkwood
corkwood	Confetti tree
Cottonwood	Cottonwood
Confetti tree	Elder
Elder	False sandpaper
False sandpaper	raisin
raisin	Field maple
Grewip	Grewip
Hibiscus	Hibiscus
Horse chestnut	Horse chestnut
Knobbly	Knobbly
compretum	combretum
Large fever-berry	Large fever-berry
Marula	Marula
Mangetti	Mullein
Mullein	Norway maple
Pine	Pine
Red flowered	Red flowered
kurrajong	kurrajong
Sage brush	Saguaro rib
Saguaro rib	Sotol
Sotol	Sycamore
Sycamore	Sycamore fig
Sycamore fig	Trumpet thorn
Teasel	Willow
Trumpet thorn	
Willow	

bow drill. For the hearth, you can use the same wood as you've chosen for the drill, or other good hearth woods such as sycamore, willow, clematis, acacia, juniper or cedar. Twirl the drill between your palms to establish a depression in the hearth and carve a notch into it in exactly the same way as you would for the bow drill.

To make fire, place an ember pan under the notch, secure the hearth board to the ground with your foot and begin drilling by rotating the drill between your palms with a steady downward pressure. As you do so your hands will travel down the drill. When you reach the end keep the drill in place as you reposition your hands at the top to begin again. Spitting into your palms and rubbing them together will help your grip. Try not to press your hands together too hard, as this will cause blisters. Concentrate instead on an easy movement for a smooth, fast drilling action. At first, as you warm the drill up, go slowly; then steadily increase your speed and downward pressure. Watch the hearth notch as it fills with powder. The hand drill produces an ember in the same way as the bow drill from which point onwards the process of making a fire is identical. When you have an ember, smoke will begin to rise from beneath the powder which will darken to black.

Saw and flexible sawing thongs

With this firestarter the friction is produced by a wooden saw or thin creeper against a hearth board of 90 degrees to the grain. These fire sets, usually made from bamboo, are a remarkably quick and efficient means of creating fire in the tropics. All you need is a parang and some suitable bamboo. Choose a piece of dead bamboo over 5cm in diameter with a reasonably thick wall. Cut out a section bearing two nodes and about half of each of the straight sections above and below them. Split this in half and break a third one off one of the halves. Make a narrow notch in the

straight drill of the right kind of wood, you can fit a short section of the correct wood to a long, straight piece of another variety. Carve the end of the drill in the same way as for the

Supporting the saw as firmly as you can by leaning on it, or by pinning it to the ground, position the hearth on the saw's edge and rub it up and down. When you notice smoke rise, rub and apply greater force. In tropical rainforest you will now be sweating profusely. Try not to let the drops fall on to the working parts of the saw. If you have prepared everything and have pitched the intensity of your effort at the right level you should be able to stop sawing after about thirty seconds. Blow through the hearth hole: if you have managed to light the shavings you should see a plume of smoke streaming from the other side of the hearth. Keep blowing until the tinder bundles have begun to glow. It might be necessary to loosen the ember from the hole with a small pick of bamboo. Once the tinder bundles are glowing, remove them and blow them to life.

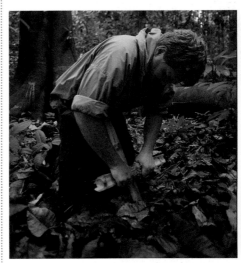

Using bamboo fire saw in Costa Rica rainforest.

outside of the shorter stick at 90 degrees to the grain and carve into it until you have a small hole 3–4mm long and 1mm wide, through the bamboo. On the inside carve a shallow groove in line with the grain. This will be the hearth.

Taking the longer piece of bamboo, carve one edge like a knife blade for the saw. Then, using your parang, scrape off the shiny outer coating of the wood in a back-and-forth action so that you finish up with two bundles of shavings, one at either end. When these are approaching the size of a hen's egg remove them and put one on each side of the hole on the inside of the hearth. Hold them in place by skewering them through the hole with small sections of green bamboo.

Fire plough

The fire plough is found along the Congo River and in Polynesia.

To construct one, start by carving a flat surface on the hearth stick. Shave up a curl of

Fire plough in use on the banks of the Congo.

wood, then begin ploughing, very slowly at first, gradually increasing your speed and rotating the plough slightly on each stroke. The action will form a longitudinal groove and produce a fibrous, dark powder against the curled shaving. Be careful not to break apart the pile of powder that forms as you plough: this will become the ember.

Transfer the ember into the fibres in a dry half-coconut husk, which will act as your tinder bundle.

Completed tinder bundle ready to go; store this in a warm dry place (for example tucked inside your clothing).

Tinders for friction firestarting

All of the friction firestarting techniques produce a small ember of fine, scorched wood dust. To convert this ember to flame you must nurture it in a bundle of tinder. This can be any flammable, dry, fibrous material to hand: grass, inner and outer barks, lichens, coconut husks, webbing material from the base of palm fronds, fine wood shavings. Rub the tinder vigorously between your hands to make it as

Clematis bark being buffed to make it soft and fine.

fine as possible. If you can, improve the bundle by placing even finer combustible material, such as plant downs, in its core. A good tinder bundle will be about the size of a grapefruit when tightly compressed. Good tinders for friction firestarters include: plant downs (as for sparks – see page 84); fungi (as for sparks – see page 84); grasses (most fibrous grass leaves); outer bark of clematis, cinquefoil, honeysuckle, red cedar, juniper, willowherb; inner bark of lime, sweet chestnut, oak, willow (dried and beaten); hairs from mature ivy stem.

Fire by chemical means

Fire can be started by various chemicals, of which perhaps only one combination is ever likely to be available to you in the wild. If you have a glycol-based antifreeze and some potassium permanganate, you can easily produce fire. Add a tablespoon of the antifreeze to a bundle of tinder, then sprinkle a teaspoon of potassium permanganate on to this, compress the bundle and put it down very quickly – on a warm day you may get a fast reaction. The two chemicals will generate enough heat to set the bundle glowing. If the reaction is occurring slowly, don't be tempted either to pick up the bundle or to walk away and leave it. Treat it as if it were a live firework. An old-time favourite disinfectant of overland travellers – it can be diluted in water to disinfect wounds and suspect salad ingredients – potassium permanganate can also be mixed with sugar, nine parts chemical to one part sugar, and rubbed vigorously between two rocks to create sparks.

Fire by electrical means

If you have either a head torch with a fresh battery or a car battery you can create sparks to start a fire.

To use a head torch, you will need some wire wool from a vehicle repair kit. Lace this

with plant downs and other fibrous tinder material and place the bundle against the battery terminals of the torch. It will glow: blow on it to ignite the tinder.

To use a vehicle battery, disconnect it and connect jump leads to the terminals. Prepare some tinder, perhaps teased-apart field dressing from the car's first-aid kit. Hold the crocodile clips by their insulators and touch them together: bright sparks will ignite the dressing and, indeed, most spark tinders.

FLAME TO FIRE

Having conjured a flame, we next need to know how to turn it into a fire, and firelighting is a skill that takes practice.

To burn properly, a fire needs three components: HEAT, FUEL and OXYGEN

Heat: Whichever firelighting technique you are using, the more heat you start with, the more certain you will be of success. In warm weather fires start fairly easily, whereas in conditions of extreme cold you may have to warm your tinder inside your clothing to produce an initial flame.

Fuel: Fuel should be carefully selected and graded by size. All kindling should be from the driest wood you can find, ideally small sticks caught in branches a safe distance away from the dampening effects of the ground. As the fire starts, add fuel gradually, small, thin kindling to start with, then thicker wood. If you add bulky wood too soon the fire will die.

Make sure you pack the fuel closely enough to allow the flame to pass from one stick to another, otherwise it will burn out in the middle, leaving the top layers unscorched.

Oxygen: Oxygen is ever present, but it can be accidentally occluded if you pack the fuel too tightly. Fire prefers to grow upwards, so flat piles of fuel burn slowly and tend to smoulder.

Avoid going too far the other way though, and ending up with something that looks like a tepee. As a general rule, build your fire from the bottom up, arranging the sticks in a criss-cross formation which will leave the necessary air spaces between them and at the same time allow gravity to ensure that they are fed into the flames.

Firelighting
Small sticks
Begin by laying down a small platform of dry, dead wood about the thickness of your thumb. This will keep the tinder and kindling off the damp ground, insulate it in extreme cold and

How to lay a fire – note platform and length of small sticks.

help it to burn quickly to provide your fire with a strong heart of embers. Lay two generous handfuls of small kindling crosswise on top of this platform. These should be no thicker than a match and about 30cm long. Do not be tempted to break them in half to cut down the time it takes to create thick bundles. Place your tinder under the sticks where they cross and ignite it.

As the fire get under way, adjust the position of the stick bundles so that they cross directly over the flames, then leave them alone. All being well, you will see a rapidly accelerating plume of smoke rise from your fire, followed shortly by flames reaching

through the bundles. At this point add a handful of pencil-thick fuel. When the flames appear through this, progress to finger-thick and kindling and continue to increase the size of the fuel until you are burning wood of the desired thickness.

In very damp weather, or when it is raining, you may find your fire takes a little while to get going, but don't interfere with it: many a fire has been stifled by too much attention. Keep an eye on the smoke: if it is accelerating, leave the fire to develop at its own pace. If, however, the smoke is petering out, take action. You may be able to adjust the fuel and increase the oxygen supply, but the likelihood is that you will have to start again. If you can develop the habit of making your preparations carefully the first time, you should see your fire roar to life in no time.

Feather sticks

After prolonged rainfall, or in an unfamiliar environment, it may be quickest to light your fire with feather sticks. Search for a suitable piece of dead, standing wood that can be split down and shaved into feather sticks as described on page 48. As with a small-stick fire, lay a platform and, using a thumb-thick piece of fuel wood, prop up the feather sticks so that their shavings face towards you, leaving a small space at their base to insert a match.

Split wood and birch bark

In regions where birch bark is abundant it can be used to ignite split wood. Prepare a platform then lay two split sticks in an upside-down V shape, crossing one stick above the other where they meet. Fill the centre of the V with birch-bark strips, ignite them and criss-cross small sticks across the top.

Dry grass

An African variation. Collect a good handful of long, dry grass stems and bind them together into a giant spill. It can be used to light quite large sticks.

Old fire dogs

The sticks left with partially burned ends after a fire has gone out can often be reignited with sparks, a friction-produced ember or any small flame. As long as they are dry, fire dogs can be relit months after they were last burned. Once a fire dog begins to glow blow on it and the ember will spread to another dog laid alongside it. Once you have three on the go you can usually start your fire anew. Incidentally, this is also a good means of starting a fire from another. Take three logs that are burning well and combine them with a bundle of fine kindling to light the second fire.

HARD WOODS FOR ROASTING	SOFT WOODS FOR BOILING
Apple	Alder
Ash	Aspen
Beech	Cedar
Birch	Hawthorn
Sweet chestnut	Horse chestnut
Hazel	Lime
Holly	Pine
Hornbeam	Poplar
Larch	Spruce
Oak	Sycamore
Willow	

Choosing your fuel

A sound can sometimes be heard in the woods late at night that indicates the presence of novice backwoodsmen: that of sticks being broken for firewood. The proficient bushcraft practitioner anticipates his or her needs before it gets dark. Choose the type of firewood you collect carefully, because different woods burn at different speeds and provide varying quantities of heat output.

Firewood must in general be dead, dry wood. Avoid picking up firewood from the ground: the best is wood caught in other branches. The more vertical its position, the drier it will be. Damp wood will burn poorly and produce too much smoke for a comfortable camp. It will also burn cold: much of the fire's energy will be expended on drying out the fuel.

Bear in mind what you will be using your fire for and how long you will need it. For warmth and most campfire cookery you'll require fuel that burns slowly and gives out a lot of heat: for a quick fire to boil the kettle, which will burn to ashes rapidly, look for a wood that burns swiftly. The old adage, 'soft woods for boiling, hard woods for broiling' –

broiling being grilling or barbecuing – still holds true.

Pine for kindling

Pine is one of the best natural kindlings. The stumps of old, dead pines are often rich in resin. Known as fat pine, or ocote in Central America, they can be chopped into splints

which ignite readily and burn well. Similar to this are pine knots: the base of branches, which can be struck from old pine logs with the poll of your axe or a heavy stick. Use them as fuel or save them to add to the fire when more firelight is called for.

Lighting pine kindling with a liquid butane lighter.

Dung

In treeless lands, nomadic peoples often use dried dung from herbivorous livestock as their main fuel. Beware the scorpions that often rest under it.

MANAGING A FIRE

Fire can be our most valuable resource, but given its capacity for destruction it can also be our greatest enemy, scarring landscapes and decimating forests.

The first question we should ask ourselves is whether or not it is appropriate to light a fire. The campfire in particular is a matter of fierce debate. One view is that hike stoves should be carried into the wilderness and used instead, because they leave behind far fewer traces of our presence. On the other side,

back-to-nature campers maintain that sitting by a campfire brings them closer to nature in a spiritual way that is impossible with a hike stove.

It all depends on where you are. It is certainly true that there are areas where the use of a campfire is inappropriate: places where it may trigger a forest fire, where fuel is not sufficiently plentiful, or where fires have never been lit before. In these regions a hike stove is a sensible option as it safeguards the environment we have set out to enjoy. But at the same time there are many other places where the flames do not threaten the forest, where fuel is abundant and where, with proper management, a campfire need not leave any unwelcome after-effects.

I recommend aiming to travel through the landscape like a shadow, leaving as little trace of yourself and your activities as possible, and to use either a campfire or a stove as your location and circumstances dictate.

Siting and clearing away a fire

When you want to build a fire, don't choose an obvious beauty spot – a scenic riverside meadow, for example: search out a quiet, concealed area that will give you some privacy and where you and your fire won't impinge on others. Avoid combustible vegetation, peaty soil and deep pine needles. What you need is a clear area with mineral soil that can be revealed by brushing back the humus, the kind of place frequently found under the dark canopy of broad-leafed woodland. It should provide shelter from wind and rain and an abundant supply of dead wood or dry dung for fuel. Always build your fuel on level ground, without digging a fire pit unless absolutely necessary; in a survival situation, you may need to make a shallow, bowl-shaped pit where you can keep a supply of embers so that you don't have to relight your fire. Never place the fire on top of exposed roots or against a tree, rock or cliff face. Keep the fire as small as possible. There is no point in

surrounding it with rocks: this won't do anything other than blacken the rocks.

Bear in mind when you intend to break camp so that by the time you leave you have fed all your fire dogs into the fire and burned them to ash, the most easily cleared byproduct of a fire. If this isn't possible, open the embers of your fire to allow them to cool and move the remaining firewood outwards, isolating each stick from its neighbour. The embers should then go out. This process can be hastened by pouring water over them and mixing it in with a stick until no steam or smoke rises. Ensure that any charred sticks are well doused. Then put the ashes into your cookpot, remove them to a good distance and scatter them widely. You should now be left with mineral earth. Use a light, dead-stick brush to spread the original humus over this so that the site blends in with the surroundings as you go. Have a last check for any litter that may have escaped your notice.

Underground roots can catch light and smoulder like a fuse, eventually surfacing to cause a forest fire. Coniferous trees, especially larches, are particularly susceptible to this. If you are in an area with soft soil, perforate the earth with a sharpened stick and pour in copious quantities of water. If you have set up camp on grassland it is best not to light a fire, but if circumstances leave you no alternative you can minimise its impact by lifting some turf and digging down to the mineral soil. Make your fire pit much larger than your fire to avoid scorching the grass at the pit edge. I usually turn over smaller pieces of turf at the rim and form a soil border around the pit, which I keep well watered. Keep the lifted turf in a shady place and water it morning and evening. When you have finished with your fire, extinguish it, remove all of the ash and embers and rake the ground to soften it. Search around for some well-weathered animal dung and place this in the pit, water it into a slurry and replace the turf. Water the

site of the fire as well. The ground should then recover quickly from its effects.

In forests carpeted with mossy peats fires are a particular risk, because the forest floor is combustible. In Scandinavia, where such conditions predominate, fires are built in to minimise the danger. Even using this method, though, you should still lay a fire only if plenty of water is available and the weather hasn't been dry for a long time. Lift the moss to a depth that will create a fire circle larger than the fire you will be setting. Put the moss in a shady place and keep it watered. Saturate the ground in your fire circle with water, and then line the pit with rocks. Lots of small rocks are better than one large one as they provide better air flow at the fire base. Don't use rocks from a riverbed; if they are saturated they will explode when heated, choose the driest you can find. Light your fire on top of the rock platform, which, once hot, will warm and improve the fire's performance. When breaking camp allow time for the fire to cool. Soak the site and lift the cold ashes and embers by hand for dispersal. Remove the cold rocks and scatter them well.

Ensure that the ground is not alight as peat fires are especially prone to smouldering underground along roots for weeks before eventually surfacing and igniting the forest. Take a sharpened stick and poke it into the ground to a depth of 30cm in and around the fire site, and pour generous quantities of water into the holes so that it penetrates deep into the peat layers, extinguishing any burning. Once you are satisfied that the fire is well and truly out, and there is no steam or smoke rising from any of the holes, replace the peat and moss that you originally moved.

Adapting your fire to your requirements

Once the fire is alight, the formation can be adjusted to suit the conditions and the uses to which you want to put it. The following are just a few examples.

Criss-cross fire lay: Built upwards, like a low matchstick tower, enclosing a base platform, tinder bundle and kindling with layers of fuel criss-crossed at 90 degrees above them. It burns well and settles efficiently to provide a deep bed of embers for cooking. It also throws out a good deal of heat so is a good design to lay in advance if you are going to need your fire to keep warm.

Criss-cross fire lay.

The leaning criss-cross fire lay: This is the method I usually choose to enlarge my fire, placing layers of firewood so that their lower ends are on the ground and their top halves criss-cross in layers above the fire. It is a stable arrangement that allows gravity to feed the fuel into the fire, leaving ends protruding so that the fire can easily be converted into a convenient arrangement.

Siberian fire lay – split wood and birch bark.

The Indians' fire: The most useful of all designs, this simple fire is ideal for

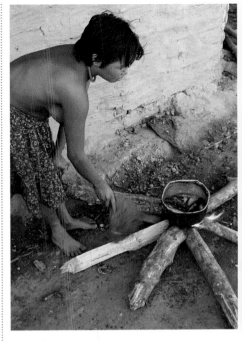

Indians' fire, Sanema, Venezuela.

backcountry travellers. Lay the wood so that it points into the fire heart in a star shape. As the fire consumes the sticks they are gradually fed into the centre. It is easily modified, enlarged and extinguished – all you need to do is to open out the star. It is particularly well suited to use with a pot-hanger (see page 36).

The star fire: This variation on the Indians' fire comprises three, or more usually four, thick logs of equal diameter. Because the logs are uniform, a pot can be supported on the burning ends meeting in the middle. This is a good fire for maintaining a supply of water in a fixed camp.

The long-log fire: The traditional fire for open-fronted bivouacs in cold weather. Using long logs supported by smaller ones, you can build a fire that stretches the length of your

Siberian fire lay – split wood and birch bark.

body and provides enough heat to keep you warm in the coldest weather. It will burn efficiently and requires minimal tending. The little supporting logs can be green wood. In the far north in winter, birch trees have such a low moisture content that once a fire has a good ember bed they can be burned green, producing a slow-burning fire with an excellent output of heat.

Tepee fire lay: As the name suggests this is a design that is tepee-shaped; the lay most often shown in illustrations of campfires. It is not, however, one I ever use. It burns quickly,

Tepee fire.

giving plenty of light, but tends to be unstable. It can also fail to feed itself by becoming lodged so that the middle burns out without igniting the upper layers.

The long log fire.

Special circumstances

There may be times when you need to make some key modifications to your fire to cope with unusual conditions or circumstances.

Windy weather: Wind can be a great problem. In hot weather, a strong gust may blow flames, sparks and even embers into surrounding vegetation. Unless there is no risk of starting a catastrophic conflagration, avoid lighting a fire in hot weather. Strong winds in cold climates will make your fire burn quickly. In these conditions use double or even treble the amount of kindling when building your fire to ensure that a lasting bed of embers forms. Then add fuel – slow burning as far as possible – placing it on the downwind side of the fire.

Wet weather: Just before bad weather the smoke from your fire may cling to the ground rather than rising into the sky. In wet weather you will need to use extra kindling and in very wet conditions, all the fuel you collect will carry moisture. To counteract the effects of this, build a larger fire than you would in

dry weather and dry out the firewood you are adding at the same time: a normal-sized fire will go cold every time you add more fuel as the fire's warmth diverts into drying it out. Splitting firewood improves its combustion.

Extreme cold: Extreme cold will slow down your fire and make it smoky. Make sure that it has excellent ventilation and that you maintain a good bed of embers. The extra clothing we wear in this weather can insulate us from the warmth of a fire as well as from the cold: take care not to scorch or melt it by standing or sitting too close to the campfire.

On snow: Always clear away the snow to the ground, make enough space to give you room to work, then insulate the ground with boughs. It is important to keep snow off your clothing and footwear when you are near to the fire or you will quickly become soaked.

If you can't clear the snow, try improvising a platform from green wood. It will eventually sink into the snow, but in the meantime it may suffice until you are able to create a better site.

No smoke: For a smokeless fire you need to use small pieces of absolutely dry wood with the bark removed. There will be a little smoke when you light it, but this will clear to a bright smoke-free fire. Keep it well constructed in a loose, upright tower. If the fire collapses, it will smoulder.

No smoke, no flame: The best method of producing a fire without smoke or flame is to

To effect rescue, signal fires must have two parts: 1. A quick-burning, heat-generating section | 2. A smoke generator of green boughs.

burn charcoal. This can be found on fire sites left by careless campers or on the tree stumps left from forest fires. The most efficient way to burn charcoal is in a brazier, which can be improvised from an empty catering tin. This is an ideal fire for cooking. For a basic brazier, simply punch some holes in the sides of the tin; for a more sophisticated version, ventilate the base and adapt the rim to support your cooking pot. Silent and smoke-and-flame free, these stoves are a delight to use, excellent for deep-frying or stir-frying with a wok. You can even press them into service as a makeshift barbecue. They will also burn twigs and dung, although not without producing smoke.

Stir-frying in a wok over a basic brazier.

Portable fires
You can keep a fire going overnight by adding firewood and then, when it is burning, excluding the air supply by covering with ash or mineral soil. In the morning expose the embers, add tinder and kindling and restart the fire, blowing if necessary.

If you are forced to move on and need to carry fire with you, follow the example of the Mbayaka pygmy – and the European 'ice man' of 5000 years ago. Wrap a few good embers or a glowing bracket fungus, in green leaves and other insulating material, and carry them in a bag, basket or similar container.

SHELTER

The primary aim of any shelter is to protect us from environmental conditions that threaten our well-being. From the moment you perceive a need for shelter, you must ensure that what we construct is appropriate to the circumstances. Ideally it should not only shield you from environmental hazards, but also provide a refuge where you can comfortably rest and recharge your batteries.

SHELTER PRINCIPLES

Probably the most common mistake made with shelter-building is to leave it too late. Shelters are most easily and effectively erected while you still have plenty of energy.

In building your shelter, remember one of the golden rules of bushcraft: maximise efficiency with minimum effort. Accordingly, your first consideration should be to position it close to necessary resources and away from hazards, and the second to construct it to a quality appropriate to its intended lifespan or to your own energy level. Successful shelter-builders think like engineers. At the design stage, they establish what the shelter is intended to provide protection against, which determines the choice of site, guides the search for materials and ultimately dictates the shelter design. To put this approach into practice you need to be aware of the physical threats the environment can present and the range of possible responses to them.

Below: Left open at the sides for ventilation, this shelter made from whale bones on Namibia's skeleton coast provides shade and some insulation.

In the cold and wet it is tempting to just sit and shiver. Instead act to improve your circumstances by reducing heat loss.

Heat loss

In cold conditions we lose heat through a number of different processes. If this is left unchecked, your body will eventually lose heat faster than it can generate it. Unless protected by clothing and/or shelter, it will lose heat to the surrounding environment at temperatures lower than 25 degrees Celsius. This will lead to a lowering of the internal core temperature and, if ignored, may result in hypothermia and, finally, death.

Radiation

Radiated heat is transferred by electromagnetic waves from warm to cool objects. We lose up to 65 per cent of our total heat through this process alone. Radiated body heat warms the cool air or moisture around us, which is then stripped away by conduction or evaporation. Radiated heat loss is greatest from exposed skin, particularly on areas of the body with a large blood supply, and the head and neck, where blood vessels are not as well insulated and our ability to reduce heat loss by vasoconstriction – narrowing of the arteries in response to cold to reduce blood flow – is less effective. Vasoconstriction is responsible for pale skin and loss of dexterity when our hands get cold.

Radiated heat loss is best reduced by covering up, especially with hats, balaclavas and hoods. Reflective foil blankets provide no significant advantage over the cheaper and more readily available polythene survival bag.

We warm ourselves with radiated heat, either directly or by reflection – from the sun, for example, or a campfire. Your shelter can be designed to maximise your exposure to such warmth and you can adapt your fire to emit radiated heat into the shelter by placing a reflector on the opposite side of the fire to bounce the heat in your direction.

Convection

The body constantly heats the layer of air or moisture next to its surface. When this layer is disturbed by cold air passing across it – the wind, for example – the heat is lost by convection. This effect is substantially reduced by windproof clothes and bivouac bags.

In shelter construction you can minimise convection heat loss by choosing a site that affords as much natural wind protection as possible. A second defence is to make the shelter draught-free. In barren wilderness devoid of trees, you will have to carry some form of windproof shelter with you.

The classic sources of convected heat are a campfire or a tent equipped with a wood-burning stove, space-heater or firebox.

Conduction

Conducted heat is heat transferred by direct contact between one object and another. The rate at which body heat is lost by this process is determined by the conductivity of the material with which we are in contact.

Rates of conducted heat loss

Air	0
Wool	1.4
Wood	4
Nylon	8 – 10
Water	23 – 25
Ice	86
Steel	1,700
Aluminium	9,300
Copper	15,000

Therefore, aluminium is 100 times more conductive than ice, steel 20 times and copper 175 times.

For example, if two climbers, each dressed identically and wearing thin gloves, are digging a snow cave, one with an aluminium shovel the other with a wooden-handled shovel, the climber using the aluminium shovel will be losing heat from his hands 2000 times faster than his colleague. This means he will become exhausted more quickly and be more prone to cold injuries, such as hypothermia and frostbite.

To reduce conducted heat loss, insulate your body from a cold surface by placing a poor conductor of heat between you and the ground. In a shelter this means erecting a bed that raises you clear of the ground. Alternatively, you might arrange some sort of underfloor heating, with warmed rocks, for example. Remember that all heat loss needs to be replaced with calories from your food supply. Canny cold-weather adventurers pay constant attention to the surfaces with which they are in contact. For example, if they are taking a rest, they might place a few spruce boughs on top of a cold rock before sitting down on it.

Evaporation

To change from liquid to gas, water requires energy. When we sweat, or when moisture in our clothes evaporates, the fluid draws energy from body heat to make the transformation. In hot weather this type of heat loss can keep you cool – by wearing a jungle hat dipped in water, for example – but in cold climates it works against you.

Water conducts heat 23–25 times faster than air: the first consequence of sweating in cold weather is an associated loss of insulation and an increase in conducted heat loss as the warm air trapped between the layers of your clothing is replaced by sweat. Then, as the wet kit dries on your body, heat is lost by evaporation.

To reduce the effect of evaporative heat loss you must strive to remain dry. Wear effective waterproof clothing and maintain an even body temperature by adjusting the layers of your clothing according to the ambient temperature and your level of physical activity. For instance, remove some layers of clothing before the physical exertion of building your shelter so that you have warm, dry things to wear when at rest. As for the shelter itself, you may design it to trap warm, dry air inside. If not, at least you should be able to dry clothes beside a campfire.

Respiration

As we breathe in cold air we warm and humidify it. When we exhale, we expel heat. This loss of warmth increases in the dry atmosphere of extreme cold environments, where more energy is used during the humidification process. Stay alert to the depletion of warmth. Aim to create a warm-air environment inside your shelter. Once again, a heated tent is advantageous.

Metabolism

As we metabolise our food to create warmth, we are using up energy. Although this process does not in itself cause heat loss, if expended energy is not replaced we become exhausted and cannot generate the necessary internal heat to stay alive. Exhaustion is a major contributor to hypothermia in outdoor activities: high energy output in cold or wet weather may require greater food supplies than anticipated. This is a key factor in mountain walkers becoming lost in bad weather. Even if clad in the most efficient outdoor clothing they are often too exhausted to stave off the effects of the cold.

It is vital, then, to remember to keep eating. The harder we work the more food we need: when food is scarce we must work less hard.

Hypothermia

Hypothermia is the greatest hazard of the bush. It can occur in virtually any latitude on land or at sea. It is avoided by wearing appropriate clothing and staying dry, well fed and watered. Hypothermia occurs when the body loses heat faster than it can generate it, until the core is unable to maintain sufficient warmth to allow the proper function of vital organs. If unremedied, hypothermia leads to death. Essentially, there are two types of hypothermia:

- exposure hypothermia, caused by prolonged exposure to cool or cold weather, usually associated with exertion and exhaustion
- immersion hypothermia, caused by the rapid cooling usually associated with immersion in cold water.

While the symptoms of these two forms of hypothermia are similar, the treatment varies greatly.

Exposure Hypothermia

Never underestimate the risk from hypothermia. Experienced travellers in back-country areas know that when weather closes in, adjustments must be made to the programme: escape routes may need to be sought or a shelter erected to wait out bad weather conditions. Wind, wet and cold are the key environmental factors that cause hypothermia. Cold alone or a combination of any two of these factors is enough to set the cooling process in motion – wet and wind, wind and cold or wet and cold. How these environmental factors affect an individual is, to a large extent, influenced by that individual's experience. An experienced back-country traveller will be correctly clothed for the weather conditions. They will have good waterproof clothing, and will know how to wear it so that they vent out moisture as they exert themselves, adding layers as they become chilled. Staying dry is vitally important. If your clothing becomes damp you will lose moisture up to 25 times faster than if it is dry.

Fitness is also important. Obviously it is a good idea to be fit when travelling in the outdoors, but even more important than this is choosing your route to suit your fitness level.

The experienced traveller also knows that when hiking, days are long, journeys exhausting and temperatures energy-sapping: more food than normal will be needed, and shelter in some form, a tent, a wind bivvy sack and a sleeping-bag. Day hikers often omit these items, then wish they hadn't when they find themselves stranded for the night.

Leadership plays an important role in dealing with high-risk hypothermia conditions. A well-led party maintains good morale, each individual staying in touch with the progress of the whole group over their intended route. A good leader makes certain that everyone looks out for everyone else and checks for symptoms of hypothermia, so that it can be nipped in the bud. A good leader will make bold, unmuddled decisions about the route to reduce the party's exposure to bad weather. Outdoor leaders should consider it their top priority to prevent members of their party developing hypothermia: once you've had it, you will be more susceptible to suffering from it again.

Anyone suffering from an injury is more prone to develop hypothermia, as are those who are anxious or depressed. If an inexperienced leader strides ahead of the group and does not involve the others in decision-making they may become uninterested in the activity, resentful of the leader, and their morale will slip. In these circumstances the risk of hypothermia grows.

Prevention is always better than cure, and this is particularly true of hypothermia, which is difficult to rectify in the field. In your planning and preparations make sure every member has sufficient clothing, food and water with them. If you are travelling in areas that don't offer natural protection from the elements, carry with you some form of shelter. As the journey develops, maintain a keen eye on every member of the party, searching for the slightest sign or symptom of hypothermia. Act promptly to avert any worsening of the situation. Always march to the pace of the slowest member of your group, and if someone should be injured or develop signs of hypothermia, act immediately. Bear in mind that children and teenagers lose heat faster than adults because their body surface area is larger in proportion to their body mass. Ensure, too, that people are not carrying unnecessary loads. Every ounce of luxury must be weighed against its potential danger. Remember the old maxim: 'LIGHT IS RIGHT.'

If a member of your party becomes hypothermic, or you decide that you must wait out bad weather before completing your journey, you must break the processes by which your body is losing warmth to the environment.

Effects of cold on our body
When the body feels a drop in temperature it takes steps to prevent further heat loss: it restricts the flow of blood to the surface of the skin by contracting and narrowing the vessels that carry blood to the extremities – vasoconstriction. The blood that would normally go to extremities moves to the body core, helping to maintain core temperature.

Manual dexterity decreases to the point where it becomes difficult to touch the tip of the thumb to the tip of the little finger on the same hand, an important sign that steps must be taken to rewarm. Ideally before you reach this point you should have sought shelter, replaced wet with dry clothing and added insulative layers to your extremities – gloves, a hat and scarf. Because the body must maintain the blood supply from the heart to the brain for body function, the head and neck areas are particularly vulnerable to heat loss: vasoconstriction is negligible in these areas.

Vasoconstriction leads to non-freezing cold injury and frostbite. As the blood that once circulated at the extremities moves to the body core, we feel an increased need to urinate. Consequently it is easy to become dehydrated, which impedes efficient blood flow through the narrowed blood vessels, and thereby intensifies the risk of cold injury to the extremities. Respond to increased urination by drinking more, preferably warm, sweet drinks, such as hot chocolate, which is warming and calorific. Caffeine-enriched drinks help to spark up a lively mental response to circumstances.

Mild hypothermia
If we do not take steps to prevent further body cooling we will become hypothermic. It is difficult in the field to accurately monitor an individual's internal body temperature so we must look for signs that this is happening. The most obvious symptom of mild hypothermia is shivering, which occurs with a body temperature at or around 35°C. In the short term shivering is beneficial in that it is an involuntary means of producing body warmth by muscular activity. However, if we don't provide further insulation and warmth, the shivering will rapidly exhaust the body's energy supply and, in the long term, lead to rapid deterioration. If someone is shivering, do something about it.

Mood changes are also associated with mild hypothermia: look out for irritability and withdrawal.

If the body temperature drops below 35°C the casualty shows increased clumsiness, irrational behaviour and is generally confused. They may appear drunk. It is vitally important that they are handled gently, given the opportunity to rest, protected from cold and further heat loss. They must not exercise as they have insufficient energy to generate heat. Exercising to rewarm someone after such profound cooling will deepen the hypothermia. It is also vitally important that no external warmth is applied to the extremities. If you take someone in a hypothermic state into a warm room their body automatically responds to the warm environment, causing an opening of blood vessels — vasodilation — and redistribution of warm blood from the body core to the extremities. This may cause a general cooling of the body core temperature sufficient to push the person into a coma. Instead place the casualty in one or two sleeping-bags to gain maximum insulation against the cold; the shivering will generate a gradual rewarming of the body at a more natural and controlled rate. If the casualty can take liquids give them warm sweet drinks — chocolate is particularly good, with honey for maximum calories to stave off the effects of exhaustion.

Also associated with mild hypothermia — at the more extreme end of the condition, at about 33°C internal temperature — is muscle stiffness. If the casualty complains of this, monitor their pulse and their breathing, restrict all activity, encourage them to lie down with their feet slightly raised and seek urgent medical assistance.

Recent research has shown that prolonged exposure to cold, wet conditions in conjunction with a reduced calorific intake can lead to a reduction in or loss of an individual's shivering response. In this case other symptoms will be more important in early diagnosis of mild hypothermia, particularly changes in mood and loss of manual dexterity.

Severe hypothermia

The most obvious sign of severe hypothermia is the cessation of shivering. At this point the casualty's life is imperilled. Arrange urgent transfer of the patient to hospital. From this point they must not be given anything by mouth, and check that their airway remains open. If their temperature continues to drop it is likely that the semi-conscious patient will slip into unconsciousness, and may even lose response to painful stimulus. Make sure that the airway is kept open, and monitor their pulse rate and breathing rate extremely carefully. Under no circumstances should a hypothermic patient be left alone. A competent first-aider should remain with them, while the most able member of the party seeks professional assistance.

There is no effective means of rewarming a severely hypothermic casualty in the field. All the first aider can do is prevent further heat loss by protecting the casualty from the environment, providing them with the maximum amount of insulation, monitoring their vital signs and providing first aid in terms of emergency breathing — if necessary, cardiopulmonary resuscitation. At all costs the casualty must be treated gently: rough handling may cause ventricular fibrillation. If you have to move the casualty do so with their head pointing downhill to help maintain the blood pressure.

Deep hypothermia

When the body's core temperature falls below 28°C the patient is considered deeply hypothermic. They may appear dead: there are no vital signs and they are extremely cold to touch. Do not give up on treatment. Many people have recovered on rewarming: have survived after several hours of rescue breathing and CPR. A doctor cannot certify someone dead until they have been rewarmed to normal body temperature.

Immersion hypothermia

Perhaps the most dangerous aspect of falling into cold water is the gasp reflex, the first result of immersion in cold water, which often leads to panic and drowning. Second is hypothermia, which sets in rapidly. Water conducts heat from the body 25 times faster than air. For the survivor of a boating accident, energetic swimming or treading water rapidly causes exhaustion and exposure to cold: a flotation aid improves survival chances by three times.

When rescuing a victim of cold-water immersion the handling of the patient can be critical. The Royal Navy discovered that, after winching people from the sea, many subsequently died. For many years the cause was a mystery. Then a naval surgeon exposed himself to cold water immersion hypothermia, and was winched by helicopter from the sea with monitoring devices attached to his body. It was discovered that the after-drop in temperature associated with helicopter rescue was not caused, as had been suggested, by massive evaporation from the downdraught of the rotor blades, but by the loss of water pressure on the legs of the victim. When someone is lifted from the sea the removal of water pressure from the thighs and calves causes blood to flow down from the core into the lower limbs, causing a fatal reduction in the core temperature. Today when people are removed from cold water after prolonged exposure they are lifted in a horizontal or foetal position.

When we consider casualties coming out of cold water we should think of them in two categories: unconscious or conscious.

• Unconscious immersion hypothermia casualties must be given appropriate first aid following the usual ABC procedure, and evacuated to hospital for rewarming. Again, even if they exhibit all the signs of death they must be treated as a viable case for resuscitation.

• Conscious patients provide a slightly more complicated scenario. If, say, a warm, well-hydrated, well-fed individual – perhaps on a dog sled trip – falls through ice into cold water, they must be removed from the water quickly, then rewarmed and dried. If a conscious patient has had prolonged exposure in cold water, treat them as you would an exposure hypothermia casualty.

Heat gain

Contrary to what most people think, the human body is better able to withstand cold than heat stress. In hot climates as the body temperature rises we become progressively less able to work or think rationally. An increase of just 6°C can prove fatal.

The physical processes of heat exchange affect the body's performance in hot environments as well as cold ones, but they work in a subtly different way. Although our normal body temperature is 37°C the temperature of the skin is usually several degrees cooler. For this reason, when the ambient air temperature rises above 32°C we begin to absorb heat. When it exceeds the body temperature of 37°C we absorb the heat much faster. In these circumstances, keep yourself well hydrated so that the body's natural cooling mechanism is working at full capacity. This may mean siting a shelter within comfortable reach of water.

There is little that can be done to counteract warming caused by hot air, but you can prevent exacerbating matters by reducing your exposure to other sources of heat. Indeed, if you take care to minimise the effects

Dry season shelter made from paper bark, Arnhemland, Australia. The fire keeps insects away.

of these it is perfectly possible to operate efficiently. I have several times been forced to work in temperatures of 55–57°C. Although the days were tiring, I remained productive. Make sure you have plenty of water, dress to keep cool and provide yourself with full shade, such as a stretched-out tarp.

Radiation

Radiation in the form of the sun's rays is one of the most serious threats to your well-being. Not only are you hotter in the sun, but you are also at risk of sunburn. In extreme desert conditions, the sun can seem to batter you into the ground: wear a large hat and long sleeves.

Experienced back-country travellers value trees as shady resting places, but they provide only partial protection from sunburn. When siting your shelter, choose natural shade, then improve on it by giving the shelter a thick roof. If you have only fabric to work with, use it in a double layer if you can, keeping the layers 30cm apart. Bear in mind that, like the canopies of trees, thin cotton fabrics and cloud cover do not offer full protection. Be aware that the leaves of some trees, like the mopane, close at midday, reducing the tree's shade value.

Large objects, such as rocks and vehicles, that have absorbed heat can act as sources of radiated heat. Avoid resting near them during the hottest part of the day. After dark, though, they may be useful in countering the chill of a desert night.

Convection

One of the most disheartening elements of extreme heat is a hot breeze. It makes you feel as though you are living inside a fan-assisted oven. In these conditions seeking shelter from the breeze is essential, as is, yet again, an ample supply of water.

If the breeze is cooling, open your shelter to allow it to circulate. Don't take such luxuries for granted. Driving through desert, people unused to the climate often become accustomed to cool air rushing through an open window or the chill of an air-conditioning unit, only to be poleaxed by the oppressive heat they encounter when they have to dig themselves out of soft ground or change a burst tyre.

If you have a limited supply of water, balance the effects of the cooling evaporation of your sweat in breeze with the loss of water this will involve.

Conduction

We collect warmth by conduction from any object with which we are in contact that has a temperature of 32°C or above: to avoid this insulate yourself with the poorest heat conductor you can find. For example, if your 4x4 breaks down in the desert, strip out the seats to improvise an insulating bed.

Conversely, if you find a surface that is cooler than your body you can rest on it to allow heat to be conducted away from you. In deserts you can sometimes dig down to a cooler layer of ground. Or lie on a raised sheet of wrinkly tin scavenged before sunrise and placed in the shade. Be careful when picking up such items: they often harbour snakes and scorpions.

Evaporation

When moisture evaporates from the surface of our skin it carries away heat – the purpose of sweating, which is the body's natural cooling system. In hot, dry conditions you can increase evaporative heat loss by wearing soaked cotton clothing. When the risk of sunburn is not high, wear loose-fitting clothing with the sleeves rolled up to allow perspiration to evaporate.

In the hot, damp conditions of a tropical rainforest, evaporative heat loss is reduced by the high humidity in the atmosphere. Here, with one of the principal methods of cooling denied us, we must be careful not to overheat. Probably the major threat to our well-being in this type of climate is over-exertion, which causes the body to warm faster than we can lose heat. Be alert to dizziness, thirst or nausea. Where it is safe to do so, cool off in forest streams at every opportunity.

Respiration

Respired heat loss, through panting, is the main way dogs and other animals stay cool. Unfortunately, for humans, respired heat loss is negligible. Hot, dry air, like cold, dry air, is humidified as part of our respiratory process, which means that when we breathe out we expel moisture as well as heat. We lose more moisture in arid conditions than in the humidity of the rainforest.

Metabolism

Heat is a byproduct of physical effort, so in hot climates be careful not to overheat yourself by working too hard. It is sometimes safest not to work at all during the hottest part of the day. Whenever practical, follow the siesta routine practised in many hot climates, resting when the sun is at its hottest and working during the early morning and evening.

Vehicles as shelter

Planes or cars are an invaluable source of useful equipment and highly visible markers of your position but, generally, they offer poor shelter. Effectively metal boxes, they can turn into ovens in extreme heat and refrigerators on a cold night. Unless you find yourself in an exceptional situation – perhaps, say, with your car caught in a snowdrift – it is usually best to improvise a more efficient shelter alongside the vehicle, remaining close to it to improve your chance of being found by rescuers if you are in trouble.

In any event, whenever you are travelling in risky areas, stock your vehicle with survival equipment, such as plenty of water, a sleeping bag, a shovel, some food, spare parts and a means of communication with the outside world. In deserts, the golden rule of survival is NEVER LEAVE YOUR VEHICLE.

Choosing a shelter site

It would be wonderful if temperature and weather were all we had to cope with when shelter-building. But, of course, nothing is so simple in outdoors life. The location of your shelter is a vital factor: it can make the difference between a comfortable, relaxed rest and a night of torture by insects, worry, or even sudden death.

Resources

The first thing I look for when choosing my campsite are the necessary resources: wood, for the main body of the shelter; brush wood, grass or forest litter for thatching; firewood and a convenient supply of water.

The ground

If you are going to be using a tarp, search for a good piece of level, well-drained ground with trees a suitable distance apart. If you will be sleeping in a hammock, level ground is much less important than trees of the necessary strength and spacing. Wherever possible I prefer a discreet campsite that allows me privacy, and other hikers an unspoiled appreciation of the landscape. If I am setting up a camp in country where security is an issue choose a site where it is difficult for anyone to approach me undetected. Depending on the level of threat, I may wait until after nightfall before pitching camp. I certainly won't cook or light a fire.

Potential hazards

Having found what seems to be a good site, look at it from the point of view of other threats. Is the ground liable to flood? Flash floods are not uncommon: a sudden thaw of snow cover or rain in the hills can cause streams many miles away to rise suddenly. Sometimes flash floods happen so quickly that they surge like a tidal wave, bringing with them dead wood, fallen trees, boulders, mud and any other debris caught in their path.

Are there any overhangs to avoid? Both branches and rock overhangs can prove fatal. In woodland, always check above you for dead branches, so aptly named widow-makers, which may be poised to crash down in a breeze. Dead branches are a particular hazard in rainforest – in fact I can recall only one visit to rainforest where I have not heard or seen one of them drop, to say nothing of whole trees after heavy rain.

With rock overhangs, be aware of cracks and fissures that suggest the rock might shear away. In no circumstances light a fire against the wall of a cliff as the heat can trigger a rock fall.

Camping close to an ants' nest may result in premature and painful awakening. Ants can be temporarily deterred by cold ash from your fire placed around the foot of your shelter supports. If mosquitoes or biting flies are a nuisance, is there another spot where the breeze will keep them off? Is there a lot of dead wood and leaf mould on the ground? If so, think about scorpions and centipedes. It may be that you can find a clearer site. If not, knock up a makeshift brush to clear away the debris.

Are predatory animals likely to be a danger? If so, is there the wherewithal to form a thornbush stockade around the camp and sufficient firewood to keep the fire bright through the night? If you are not alone, you may be able to organise a watch rota. Have you got food or strongly scented toiletries with you that may attract a bear? If in doubt, stow them out of reach a quarter of a mile from your camp, and set your cooking facilities well away from where you plan to sleep.

Is the campsite at risk from avalanche? This is particularly important when constructing snow caves (see page 128). Never camp below a potential avalanche slope.

Is your tent liable to be covered by a snowdrift? In temperate lands we are used to pitching tents in the lee (wind-protected) side of a rock or other wind barrier. In the treeless higher latitudes of the barren Arctic, however, setting up camp in the lee of a rocky outcrop or iceberg can prove fatal in a blizzard, because snowdrifts build up in the lee side of such obstacles. In bad storms such drifts can bury tents and suffocate the occupants.

Building the ideal shelter

Let's recap on our design criteria. It should now be clear that our ideal should:

- be as easy to construct as possible
- be sited close to water and building materials
- not be sited on land liable to flood
- be away from overhanging dead branches or rock
- not arouse the interest of dangerous animals
- be away from insect pests
- keep us dry
- provide us with a raised platform or insulating bed
- in cold weather provide a warm, dry atmosphere
- in hot weather, provide shade and a cooling atmosphere

It is not, of course, always easy to fulfil these requirements. For instance, you might be injured, unable to light a fire or equipped insufficiently. However, there is a wide range

In the Siberian Taiga I recline in a classic northland lean-to. The long log fire burns the length of the shelter, keeping me warm in sub-zero temperatures without a sleeping bag.

of techniques available to us, and these can be adapted to help us cope with new or unexpected circumstances.

Making a bed

In almost all the types of shelter described in the following pages, you will need to fix yourself up with a bed of some kind, whose purpose, besides the obvious one, is to elevate the body from cold ground. The materials with which you construct it will vary according to the part of the world in which you find yourself, but dead branches and springy boughs make good, insulating bedding. Use thick, heavy boughs on the ground, topping them with increasingly fine, more comfortable layers.

It makes a big difference if these boughs can be retained within a wall of one or more long logs which can be anchored in place with wooden pegs. The so-called cot-wall bed is therefore the most popular choice for sleeping in a shelter. Make sure that your body won't sink below the level of the retaining log: if it does, you will rest in the shadow of the log and be cut off from the light and warmth of the fire.

In open-fronted lean-tos in cold weather it is usually best to create a sleeping platform at chair height.

If you are occupying your shelter on a longer term basis, it might be easier to weave yourself a blanket from natural vegetation, either by improvising a loom or by hand, which is probably the simplest and most effective way of going about it.

The simple leaf hut

One of the simplest of all shelters. Indeed, the ease and speed with which it can be erected put it streets ahead of many better-known shelters. It incorporates techniques that are used in a lot of designs and with which we are therefore likely to be familiar.

Having found a suitable site, begin by

Measure out the size of the shelter.

measuring out the shelter size: lie on the ground and mark your body length with two sticks, one at your feet and the other at your head. Next fix three main supports. Choose naturally curved fallen branches ideally with forked ends that can be interlocked at the shelter apex. These should be stout, as they will need to bear most of the thatching; always allow for the extra weight of the roof after rain. Now lean a rough lattice of fallen branches against two sides of this basic framework with the aim of creating an overall matrix that will provide a basis for a covering of forest-floor debris. This lattice doesn't have to be regular: all too often shelters are given uniform square lattices that are unnecessarily complicated and time-consuming. Concentrate instead on gearing to the kind of thatching material you are using. Make sure that the gaps in the lattice are not so large that the leaf mould can fall through, and that the ends of the sticks will not extend beyond the apex.

Starting at ground level, pile decaying debris from the floor on to the lattice, gradually working upwards in layers until the shelter is completed. Check that none of the

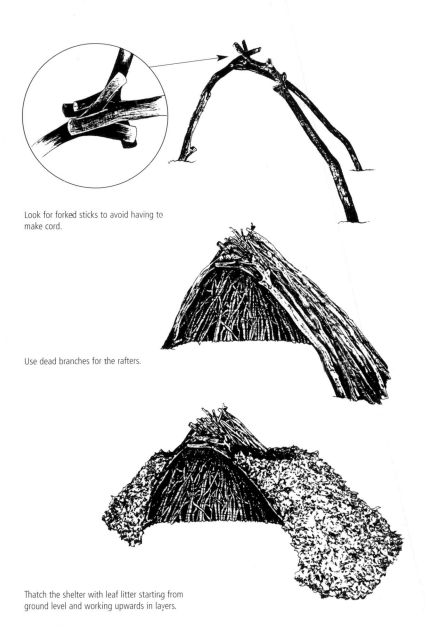

Look for forked sticks to avoid having to
make cord.

Use dead branches for the rafters.

Thatch the shelter with leaf litter starting from
ground level and working upwards in layers.

Opposite page, top: after setting up your bed, erect the shelter framework; centre – note shelter sited under tree canopy for extra
protection; bottom – this shelter is intended to be used with a fire providing warmth.

The enclosed leaf hut

supporting sticks or lattice sticks is poking through the thatch. If it is, rain will run straight down it to the inside of the shelter. The thatch should be at least 30cm deep all over. Once it is in place, anchor it against breezes by leaning a light covering of small, dead branches on top of it.

This shelter should be equipped with a cot–wall bed and a long log fire (see page 93).

The enclosed leaf hut

The enclosed leaf hut takes slightly longer to construct than the simple leaf hut and requires more accurate measurement. Its great advantage is that it does not need a fire: the design preserves your body heat to provide warmth.

Mark out your body length, then arrange a stout, strong ridgepole the full length of the shelter. Prop it up at one end with a small bipod or single forked stick set securely into the ground. This support arrangement must be very strong, as it will bear the full weight of the thatch. Allow for the extra weight of the roof after rain. It is important that the ridgepole is propped up at a height that will minimise the internal space of the shelter to maximise warmth but at the same time provide enough space for comfort. Lay down your bed at this stage so that you know it will fit inside. The only way to be sure of getting the size right is to check the dimensions of the structure continuously as you build it: the internal dimensions will shrink under the compressive weight of the thatch.

Against the ridgepole, lean a lattice of small fallen branches as you would for the simple

The two-person shelter has a good covering of leaves with inner thatch absent to show sleeping space to retain warmth.

leaf hut, ensuring that none of the sticks protrudes above the shelter apex. Allow for an opening to the shelter either at the head end or, preferably, just to one side to form a funnel-like doorway.

Like the simple leaf hut the shelter can be thatched with whatever forest debris is to hand, to a depth of at least 30cm all over: hold it in place with a light covering of small, dead branches.

Two-person shelter

The two-person shelter is a logical extension of the enclosed leaf hut – a warm shelter to use when you cannot light a fire – and only takes slightly more work to construct. Think of it as two sleeping-bags joined at the head end. As with the enclosed leaf hut, your bed should be laid down at the point where you

are testing the ridgepole height. The walls of the shelter will enclose your bedding and prevent it from spreading. Instead of one ridgepole, this shelter has two sharing the same support stick, forming a low tripod shape

Brush tepee

with one short leg and two long ones. The ridgepoles are splayed out and thatched in the same way as the enclosed leaf hut. Allow for a central entrance. In the small living space between the beds, a candle can be lit for heating – though you will need to be careful not to set the shelter alight.

Brush tepee

This is not a design I use very often, as it requires big investment in terms of labour and materials. There is a lot of thatching involved because of its height, and it needs to be thick enough to shed rain properly. Lower-roofed shelters are generally much easier to build and to make weatherproof, so I'd consider the group shelter ahead of this one. However, if in a country offering a wealth of many small branches you can use without damaging the forest, the bush tepee is a viable option.

Begin by constructing a tripod of strong, straight, mature saplings 4–5 metres in height. Lash them securely with roots or withies at the top. Whittle the ends into a point and thrust them securely into the ground to prevent the tripod from collapsing when loaded. A metre and a half from the apex, lash three crossbars to these poles. Now shorter upright poles can be leaned against this framework and the crossbars lashed into place to accept the thatching materials. Rather than attaching all the crossbars first and then thatching it is best to tie on the crossbars as you thatch. This way you use only as many crossbars as you need, and they will be correctly placed. Start thatching at ground level, ensuring that you cover the ground well to prevent draughts, and work upwards. Leave a space 80cm wide for an entrance and improvise a thatched frame for the door. Inside you can light a small fire in a wok-shaped fire pit no more than 15cm deep. The pit will help to keep the embers alight even if the fire dies low. In extremely cold snowy conditions, the bush tepee can be overthatched with snow for insulation. Remember to make a ventilation hole near ground level with a stick or ski pole to keep it open in snowstorms (see page 128).

Top: The same brush tepee design built to a larger size in Lapland.

Below: Internal view showing beds and fire pit – only a small fire is necessary to heat this shelter.

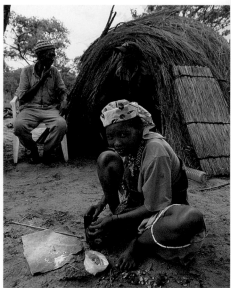

Simple but effective desert shelter breaks a cold breeze or rainfall.

Tightly woven shelter protects against rainy season storms. Note the door.

Wiltja

The shelter traditionally used by Aboriginal peoples of the Australian desert. Since few flexible saplings are available here it is usually made from mulga branches and thatched with spinifex. The basic construction is similar to the simple leaf hut, except that the shelter is much deeper, enabling several people to sleep in it side by side. The upright poles chosen for their curved shape are set securely into holes excavated with a digging stick and covered with a loose lattice of small, dead branches, which is thatched with clumps of spinifex bush. The sandy ground is carefully cleaned of any dead sticks or thorns, and if necessary a dry-grass bed is laid. At the entrance a small mulga-wood fire is lit and a windbreak is quickly put together from some dead mulga branches and more clumps of spinifex as necessary. This can be moved as the wind changes.

Wickiup

Another desert, another shelter. The wickiup was traditionally used by peoples such as the Chiricahua Apache in south-west America.

It is made up from long, flexible saplings set into the ground in a circle of holes excavated with a digging stick. The saplings are bent over and interlaced to form an upright, dome-shaped structure. This is thatched with bunches of grass kicked out from the ground and held in place with encircling bands of natural cordage or other saplings. As always, the shelter is thatched from ground level upwards. The top is finished with a good depth of thatch.

In the head-waters of the Orinoco River in Venezuela I used one of the most remarkable jungle shelters I have ever encountered. Its architects are the Sanema, and their design and technique are so efficient that, as I watched them, working in groups of six, they created overnight accommodation for fifty people in the space of thirty minutes.

To build the shelter they need to find three trees, which must be strong enough to support hammocks, growing in a triangular configuration and close enough to each other to be joined by a shelter frame. If the hunters can't locate three suitable trees they manage with two and a pole fixed firmly into the ground.

Three cross poles are then lashed with lianas to the uprights to connect them, one positioned horizontally 2.5 metres above the ground and the other two at an angle to meet at a higher point. Across this triangular frame a roof of straight sticks, about 3 metres long, is laid. A layer of overlapping wild banana leaves, anchored with a few extra sticks, is placed on top of this to make the roof waterproof. The occupants tie their hammocks in pairs, one above the other, between the three posts, so that each shelter holds up to six hammocks. Anyone who hasn't brought his hammock with him will quickly improvise one from the split lianas.

In the middle of the shelter, dead wood is feathered with a machete and a fire lit. The cooking pot is suspended over the fire with a simple pot crane. Smoke from the fire lingers in the shelter, deterring insects.

Palm-frond hut

Perhaps the most commonly encountered shelter design in the tropics is a hut with a pitched roof and a raised sleeping platform. It can be made from a wide range of materials. The framework can be of bamboo, wood, or even the midrib of palms such as the coconut palm. For the roof thatching you can use split and thatched palm fronds, sago palm leaves

Right, top to bottom:

• First a triangular frame is made.
• Next this is given long cross pieces.
• Wild banana leaves act as massive roofing tiles.
• Hammocks are stretched between the three corners.

A strong roof design lashed together with sago palm midribs.

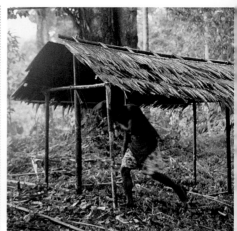

Built in one hour, this shelter will survive at least six months.

folded over a split midrib and stitched in place with a thin, flexible splint from the midrib, grasses or large, flat leaves.

Set the major uprights firmly into the ground and add a ridgepole. Next the corner posts are erected. The ends of the poles should be as level as possible. Set secondary eave ridgepoles on their tops and tie them securely in place. Lash the diagonal supports securely from the ridgepole to the eave pole. If fresh bamboo is available this is easily done: just cut a pole long enough to be bent over the ridgepole and tied down on to both eave poles. Cut out a section of the bamboo where you want to bend the pole.

Pygmy hut

The Mbayaka Pygmy of the Central Africa rainforests make small dome-shaped shelters from flexible saplings. The roof is thatched with large mongongo leaves by shaving up a sliver of the midrib into a hook, to which the leaves can be attached like roofing tiles. Inside they sometimes build a raised sleeping platform, running up a blanket from a sheet of suitable bark.

Arctic open lean-to

This shelter is geared to the great boreal forests where mainly tall, straight timber is thick on the ground, and the axe is carried as the primary survival tool. You should not build it using green wood where the cutting of such wood will cause lasting damage to the forest, as would be the case, for instance, in broad-leaved deciduous woodland.

Find two trees 2.5 metres apart aligned at 90 degrees to the prevailing wind. This angle will minimise the amount of smoke from your fire entering your shelter. In breeze-free conditions, build at 90 degrees to the slope of the ground: cooling air running downhill at night can drive in the smoke. Fix a strong ridgepole to the trees, lashing with roots or withies, or by propping it up with fork-ended branches. Next construct your bed at chair height. It must be positioned so that you sleep side on to the fire, and it must be level. Take time to get this right.

Now add the roof: lean straight poles against the ridgepole and tight up against the bed. In wet weather give the roof a very steep angle; in drier conditions the slope can be

Classic northern lean-to in Rocky Mountains. Steep roof gives best rain proofing.

At −48 °C a quinze is a welcome shelter.

gentler. In spruce forests you can use small trees for this, cleaning them of their boughs, which you can save for thatching. Finish the roof from ground level – as always – with a thatch of thick layers of boughs.

Lay some fine branches on the sleeping platform in an overlapping herringbone pattern with the soft tips at the head end to give extra depth by way of a pillow.

Finally light a long-log fire in front of the shelter, at least one full pace from the bed, and stock up on enough fuel for the night. As long as you build the fire properly its warmth will convect and radiate heat towards your body, from the side and from above, too, as it will bounce back from the roof. It will also warm you a little from underneath the sleeping platform. It is rarely necessary to use a reflector, or backlog fire, with a long-log fire. If you need extra warmth you can heat dry rocks, not rocks from rivers or damp ground which are likely to explode, as are lumps of concrete or glassy stone such as flint, in the fire, and position them with forked sticks under the sleeping platform as underfloor heating. Obviously you will have to take care

not to heat them to the point where they will cause a fire.

The quinze

The quinze is a first-rate snow shelter ideally suited to northern forests when the temperature is below −10°C. In such conditions snow remains fine, dry and powdery, and even making a snowball let alone cutting snow blocks is impossible. Instead, using shovels or snowshoes form a large mound of snow around 3 metres in diameter and 2 metres high. If there are enough of you the easiest way to do this job is in a team of three. Put one person in the centre on skis or snowshoes to trample down the snow while the other two pile it inwards. The stamping breaks the snow crystals, encouraging them to stick together in a solid mass. Once the mound has been completed, take pencil-thick sticks of equal length, about 30 centimetres, and push them into the snow at 90 degrees to the surface. In very cold temperatures you can begin to hollow out a shelter at once, although it is usually best to leave it for a while to give the snow a chance to refreeze. In the meantime have a warming drink, then collect firewood and spruce boughs for bedding insulation.

Returning to the mound, excavate the snow from ground level, carefully hollowing it out until you expose the ends of the sticks you have placed in the quinze. This will ensure that the thickness of the walls remains constant and prevent you inadvertently digging too far and weakening the structure.

Inside you must add a ventilation hole and form a raised sleeping area so that cold air sinks to below the level at which you are sleeping. Insulate the sleeping platform with plenty of spruce boughs. A candle inside the quinze will provide some warmth and a cheery light, and can prove a useful warning of an excess of carbon monoxide build-up which will make the flame sputter or even go out. Check that your ventilation hole is clear and that you have a means of keeping it that way from inside the quinze. Store your shovels inside the quinze and leave your skis outside in a place where they can easily be located if there is a heavy snowfall. Snowshoes should be hung on a nearby branch.

Spruce-tree bivouac

In deep snow in the northern forests, you can build a quick shelter by excavating a space under a spruce tree. In colder temperatures, −10°C and above, when the snow is damp and heavy, this design is less efficient than the quinze and more labour intensive because powdery dry snow is more difficult to move.

Search for a spruce with a wide spread of branches at its base and a good depth of snow all around it. If you can find the right tree to start with you are halfway there. Choose one growing on high: if you site your shelter in a gully it will fill with cold air during the night.

Dig a space between the canopy of the branches, breaking off the lower ones as necessary, to create a living area. Reinforce the lower branches of the tree with extra sticks

and boughs, piling additional snow on top to create a volcano-like wall round the shelter. Choose a side for an opening. If you are on a slope, try to ensure that the opening is facing away from the wind, looking along the slope rather than up or down it: this will reduce the likelihood of smoke filling your shelter. In the opening lay a long-log fire with a reflector behind it. Inside the shelter, clear the snow back to the ground, or as far as you can, and if possible make a sleeping platform with a spruce-bough covering. If that isn't possible fill the sleeping area of the shelter with spruce boughs taken from another tree.

Snow cave

Snow caves have saved the lives of hundreds of mountaineers caught in blizzards. The principle of digging into a snow bank to get out of the weather is so simple that these shelters have been successfully created by mountaineers with no formal instruction in how to make them. For a basic snow cave all you need to do is dig straight into the snow slope and hollow out a sleeping space to the left and right in a T shape – that's it.

A more elaborate shelter for two people can be even easier to produce. Look for a snow bank with a short slope about 3 metres deep at its top. Not only does digging your cave at the top of a slope put you in less danger of starting an avalanche, but removing the snow is easier as you can throw it down the bank behind you.

Although snow is soft, digging out a snow cave is hard work, so having the right tools for the job makes a great difference to the energy you expend and thus to your chances of survival. Most people recognise that a snow shovel is an essential piece of equipment for winter mountaineering, but you should also have a snow saw, which will enable you to cut

Opposite: Quick to construct, the spruce tree bivouac is cosy for one but cramped for more.

① ② ③

Ventilation kept open with ski pole.

Candle for warmth.

Shovel inside - in the event of a cave-in you can dig out.

Sleeping platform

3m

2m

Shelter at top of slope where avalanche risk is small.

Snow cave

out the snow in blocks with the maximum of speed and the minimum of effort. I would estimate that using a snow saw takes only a third of the energy your body would have to devote to digging with a shovel alone. As a result you will be less tired, drier and in a happier frame of mind as you work and afterwards.

Flatten the snow in a vertical face 2 metres wide by 2.5 metres high, and with your saw make two vertical incisions 60cm apart and 1.5 metres long. Connect them with horizontal cuts top and bottom to form a rectangle. Next make two vertical cuts 20cm inside your original cuts so that they meet the first vertical incisions in a wedge (1). Start to remove the snow with an upward movement of the saw, beginning 50cm below the highest horizontal incision at about 30 degrees to your last vertical cut (2). The snow should break away in wedges and slide into your gloved hands. Toss it over your shoulder so that it falls down the slope behind you and out of your way (3). Continue cutting in this way until you have taken away the snow within the rectangle to the depth of the saw blade. Then create a T shape by slicing the snow on both sides of the upright cuts, and excavate the snow until you have carved out enough space for sleeping platforms. Already you will be shielded from the weather and feeling the benefit of the shelter. Add the ventilation hole and plug the top bar of the T shaped entrance with one long block of snow and two smaller ones.

As always, store your shovel in the cave and keep a means of clearing the ventilation to hand. Place insulation beneath you and smooth the inside of the roof to prevent crests, which drip melting snow on to you. The original entrance to the cave doubles as a cold well, ensuring that the warmer air rises to the top of the shelter where you will be sleeping. Check that the roof is not too low to allow free movement because it will gradually sink under the weight of the snow. Novice snow-holers are often alarmed by this movement, which is quite normal and not a worry in itself. However, it does mean that you will be lucky to get three days out of a cave without having to increase the roof space, or make a new cave.

Snow trench

The snow trench is a quick overnight shelter suited to dry, cold conditions when you do not anticipate a heavy snowfall. It is an excellent bivouac on a cross-country journey in the boreal forest, for example. Dig a trench in the snow deep enough for you to lie in, well down out of the wind. Make it wide enough to stop you coming into contact with the walls when you turn over in your sleep. Insulate the trench with a good depth of spruce boughs, and try to arrange some simple cover at the head end to keep the snow from falling on your face – perhaps your jacket laid over crossed skis.

Fighter trench

In the mountains, where you are likely to find snow firm enough to be quarried, the snow trench can be modified and improved. Search for deep, hard-packed snow on a flat, avalanche-free surface. Test for 1m depth snow. Dig out the snow with your saw in blocks measuring 90 x 45 x 16cm. Next dig your trench, and around the inside edge of it carve out a recess to accept the base of the blocks. Cut one of the blocks into a triangular shape and stand it at the end of the trench. Cut another in half and set it on to the recess, leaning against the triangular end block. Repeat this process with the full-sized blocks, staggering the positions of the blocks as you would in brickwork, until the trench is roofed. At the point where the blocks meet, cut vertically through them and they will become perfectly bevelled and sit solidly against each other, forming an angled roof over the trench.

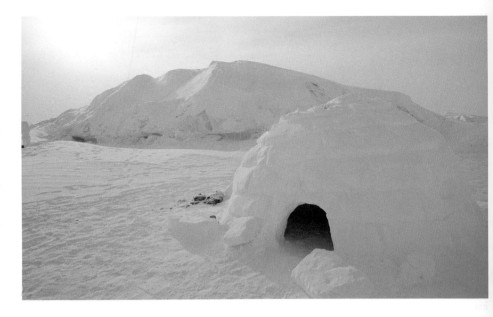

Continue until the whole trench has been roofed, block in the ends and make an entrance. If the snow is deep enough, dig a cold well in front of the entrance to collect cold air. As always, attend to the insulation beneath you, and ventilation. Keep your shovel inside the trench.

Igloo

In the high Arctic the igloo was the traditional winter shelter. Inside it was heated by a koodlik seal-blubber lantern with a wick made from cotton grass and dried moss. Today the indigenous Inuit tend to use heated frame tents, which are quick and easy to erect, along with modern sleeping-bags, stoves and space-heaters, but the art of igloo-building has not been forgotten. However, while experienced practitioners can assemble an igloo in thirty to forty-five minutes, it takes more skill and expertise than can be picked up from a book. If you are setting out into these barren northlands, go well equipped and learn igloo-building from the masters.

Group shelter

The group shelter is a more sophisticated amalgam of many of the construction techniques we have so far covered. In essence it consists of a circle of joined open-fronted lean-tos facing inwards. It is one of the best designs of all, in terms of both the effort it takes to build and its effectiveness as a temporary home, offering a warmer and more comfortable living space than any other shelter.

The ideal group shelter accommodates four people although the design can easily be adapted to suit three or a more sizeable team. I have several times built one for a group of twenty, although for this many occupants it needs to be oval rather than round and you have to factor in more space for the fire.

Begin by getting each person to lie down, end to end in a circle, and marking out his or her body length to gauge the shelter dimensions. When calculating these, allow extra space for a doorway and storage areas. The middle of each bed should be one pace from the rim of the central fire pit. Then plant your upright forked sticks into the ground. These will support the weight of the roof, so they must be strong, well dug in and all installed at the same height. Connect these sticks with short ridgepoles resting securely in the forks. If you can't wedge them in tightly, bind them in with withes. You will now be looking at a henge-like ring.

Next lean strong diagonal supports against the forked sticks, digging them into the ground at the outer edge of the sleeping space. By this stage the shelter should be pretty solid. It is important to keep it symmetrical so that it is self-supporting and won't collapse. For the roof, lay sticks diagonally against the ridgepoles and thatch the hut with forest debris, starting as always at ground level and working upwards. For the fire the opening at the apex should be 1 metre in diameter, which will allow smoke to escape even in cold weather and at the same time help to trap warm air inside.

Make a lintel for the doorway from a faggot of small sticks. This should be about 30cm in diameter and slightly longer than the length of the doorway. Restricting the height of the entrance in this way will reduce heat loss from under the shelter and help the fire to

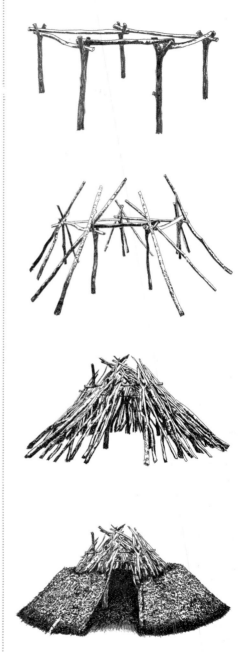

draw properly so that the interior doesn't become too smoky. Using withes, secure the lintel horizontally across the doorway at about sternum height, and thatch the roof above it. Hang a rolling blind mat over the entrance to keep the warmth in and the wind out. Inside, the sleeping area will consist of one continuous cot-wall-type bed running in a circle round the hut. Cooking pots can be positioned over the fire in pot-hangers suspended in the centre on a single wooden stick across the opening in the apex.

Complete the shelter by removing any protruding branches or sticks that may cause you injury or discomfort. If you don't do this, you are certain to regret it after dark.

Seen up close, the group shelter resembles a small volcano. Its shape naturally encourages an updraught that draws smoke away freely. If you build the shelter properly, it will be warm and cosy and space will not be too restricted;

built wrongly, it will be either cramped or cold and draughty. It does take practice and experience to gauge the dimensions to perfection. Another of its advantages is discretion. There are no obvious angles or shadows discernible from the outside and because it has been created from local debris it blends almost invisibly into the landscape, muffling the sounds made by its occupants and concealing the glow of their fire.

There are two main risks with this shelter: collapse and fire. Avoid any accidents by appointing one team member to be responsible for ensuring that it is correctly constructed at each stage. In a group of young people, the shelter captain should be an experienced adult, preferably with some training in bushcraft and first aid. It certainly shouldn't be anyone who hasn't successfully built one of these shelters before. If you have sleeping-bags you can dispense with the fire risk altogether, by not lighting one, but if you don't you will need warmth. Stay safe and comfortable by sticking to the following guidelines.

- Fires produce the most smoke and flames when they are being lit. Keep your fire small and set it into a shallow wok-like depression, which will give it a good ember base so that you won't be continuously relighting it.
- Burn only dry, dead wood to minimise smoke. Use firewood that burns long and warm, such as oak or beech.
- Make sure that water is always kept to hand inside the shelter in a place with which everyone is acquainted. The shelter captain should be responsible for this task.
- Establish an evacuation point in case of fire or any other emergency.
- If you are going to keep the fire burning through the night operate a watch system to ensure both safety and warmth.

Natural shelters

As we have seen, one of the overriding aims of bushcraft is to achieve maximum efficiency for the minimum effort. When it comes to finding shelter, this means staying alert to the possibilities that may be offered by the landscape. There are a number of natural and manmade features that might provide shelter in themselves, or could be easily adapted to do so.

Caves

Caves and rocky overhangs have given shelter for hundreds of thousands of years, but there are a few hazards of which you should be aware. Humans are not, of course, the only creatures to seek shelter in caves: spiders, snakes and even bears may view as home the one that you have happened upon. Be on the alert for tracks and other signs of such occupancy at the cave entrance. Caves heavily soiled by the guano of a large bat or rodent

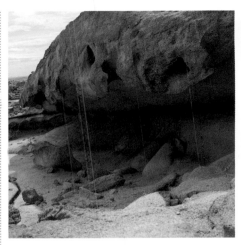
Rock overhangs provide welcome shade in arid lands, but be sure to look for snakes.

population are also best avoided. Inhaled as dust, guano can cause several dangerous diseases – histoplasmosis, hantavirus and melioidosis, to name three.

If you are sheltering from a storm, another important consideration is what is described as the 'spark-plug' effect in which lightning can pass across the gap between the cave roof and your head as it searches for the shortest route of conduction. Take the precaution of allowing at least 3 metres' clearance between your head and the cave roof.

As far as comfort is concerned, caves can be draughty. You will need to provide yourself with an insulative bed and possibly some form of windbreak.

Fallen trees

Fallen trees can sometimes be turned into shelter or incorporated into a shelter design as a wall or ridgepole. Keep an eye open for harmful creatures that may inhabit fissures in or beneath the bark. Fallen-tree shelters are difficult to make draught-proof and they can also cause complications in construction methods.

Stone walls

On moorland where few trees are to be found, stone walls may be used as a windbreak. Or, for an emergency shelter, a polythene survival bag may be pitched against a wall.

Hollows

Hollows and ground depressions have the allure of a nest, a quality that attracts many novices to build their shelters in them. But for the most part they are damp places in which to pitch camp. If you must sleep in such a place, perhaps because you need to stay hidden, search for the driest hollow you can find in well-drained ground. Lay down extra bedding or, better still, construct a raised bed and put a roof over the depression to channel away rain from its rim.

Hollow trees

Both standing and fallen hollow logs have been used as shelter. If you can find a tree with enough space in it to accommodate your body, clean it out as best you can, but stay on the lookout for venomous creatures. When you are satisfied that all is safe, crawl inside.

Sangars

In many desert areas nomadic herdsmen create sangars, small corrals with low stone walls for their sheep. These can be pressed into service as shelters with a tarp or other improvised roof spread across the top. Before moving in, clear out any rocks or dung. Watch out for scorpions, which like to live underneath both dung and rocks.

Useful equipment for natural shelters

Polythene survival bag: On a mountain expedition it is best to take with you emergency survival gear such as a sleeping mat, Gore-tex bivvy bag and warm clothing or a lightweight sleeping-bag. However, many mountaineers rely on the lightweight polythene survival bag. If you need to use one of these as an emergency bivouac, put on whatever spare clothes you have with your waterproof clothing on top and search for a large rock, rocky outcrop or stone wall to shelter behind. Improvise some ground insulation: for example, sit on your climbing rope. At the closed end of the poly bag, cut a small face hole to breathe through. Pull the bag over your body, put your feet inside your rucksack for further insulation and eat some of your emergency food. Keep your whistle and torch to hand for signalling.

Portable bothy: An improvement on the polythene bag, which is available in a range of sizes to accommodate from two to six people. This lightweight, portable shelter made of waterproof Dayglo-orange nylon and fitted with ventilation holes provides instant protection from wind and rain. Warmed by the body heat of the occupants, it is surprisingly comfortable. To gain maximum benefit from the bothy use it in the lee of a wall or large boulder and, as with the poly bag, insulate yourself from the ground with rucksacks or climbing ropes.

Polythene sheeting: If you have some polythene sheeting available you can improvise all manner of shelters. The only major drawback to using polythene is that because it is totally impermeable, condensation will build up inside and may soak your dry, insulative layers. Try to keep your bedding away from the shelter walls and make sure you have enough ventilation for the condensation to evaporate.

Parachutes: Ex-military parachutes can often be bought in army surplus stores. They may no longer be serviceable as parachutes, but have many good years ahead of them as lightweight shelter. There are ways without end to pitch parachutes as shelters, and the fabric can be adapted to produce a variation on many of the shelters we have already looked at. The key point to remember is that parachute nylon is not waterproof so it won't offer protection from the rain used any old how. But stretching taut improves its capacity to shed rain, and arranging it in two layers 30cm apart virtually guarantees a dry shelter. Parachutes can also be cannibalised for their nylon cord and the

nylon cord can be used in turn for its fibres, which can be used for fishing-line or sewing thread.

The suspended parachute tepee is the option I usually go for. Stretch the parachute fairly taut, high off the ground in a single layer. This gives you an excellent shelter to work under, and although it isn't fully rainproof it breaks the force of the rain.

Lightweight trail shelters

One of the greatest joys of travelling in remote regions is the sense of independence and freedom it gives you. To enjoy such nomadic wandering you need an easily transported shelter. My preference, for many reasons, is a lightweight tarp or shelter sheet. It is light, weighing as little as a kilogram, which increases your capacity for extras such as a warmer sleeping-bag or more food. It is versatile, providing all kinds of protection, from shade in arid zones to shelter from the rain in the tropics. Also under a tarp you sleep close to nature and wake up to limitless fresh air. A tarp shelter can be pitched in moments, then taken down and packed away just as quickly.

Fixed-tarp shelter

I opt for the fixed-tarp shelter only when I plan to be pitched for more than a few days. I usually fasten two tarps together to give myself more room for manoeuvre for the duration. You could do the same if you are travelling with others: this combined shelter will comfortably sleep two or three people.

Cut forked uprights and one strong ridgepole to fit the dimensions of your tarp and set the upright supports in the ground a tarp length apart with the ridgepole between them. Pop together your tarps, pitch them over the ridgepole and peg them taut to the ground. If your tarps don't fasten to each other, pitch one of them on one side allowing 15cm to overhang the ridgepole and peg it out with guy lines on both sides. Do the same with the tarp on the other side so that both tarps are stretched taut, overlapping at the ridgepole.

You can make the shelter more snug by enclosing the ends with simple thatching. Fully thatch one end, doing only half the other to leave a space for the doorway. Set short, upright wands into the ground, green-stick-fracture them at the tarp edge, and bend the tops down to rest just under the tarp. The ends can be interwoven to provide structural support. Interweave horizontal withies, bending down their ends, and dry grasses or plants, or other thatching materials.

Simple tarp bivouac

This commonly used shelter is particularly suited to forest camping, and gives you an enriching sense of closeness to your environment. The secret is to have your tarp already set up with appropriate guy lines so that you can pitch it easily after dark.

Among the usual criteria we apply to finding the right site, protection from the prevailing wind is a particular priority for using the tarp bivouac. Look also for an area where the trees are wide enough for you to set up your tarp between them. Pitch the tarp at about the height of your sternum (lower in very bad weather, or if you wish to keep a low profile) and peg it out with simple improvised pegs. In country which is home to insects and venomous snakes it is a good idea to pitch a mosquito net beneath your tarp. Choose one with a sewn-in groundsheet that can be zipped up.

Tarp-and-hammock bivouac

The tarp-and-hammock is my favourite way bar none of sleeping outdoors. I use this bivouac in the warm months of the year in temperate climates and most of the time in the tropics. Search for two trees at a suitable distance away from each other to take your hammock and tarp, and pitch the tarp at a height of about 2m, guying it out firmly. Tie up your hammock beneath it, with or without a mosquito net, depending on the conditions. I string a cord between the tarp and the hammock where I can hang my clothes and boots overnight. The whole operation takes only five minutes, and when you break camp in the morning there is hardly a trace that you were ever there, which is the perfect way of camping in forests.

Evenk slippery figure-of-eight hitch.

This is the method used by Evenk reindeer-herders of Siberia to tie a strong quick release hitch. It is one of the most useful knots – excellent for tying up taut lines.

Tarp taut hitch.

Used to tie and tighten the ridge cord of a tarp shelter tightly and securely, it releases with a pull on the working end.

The slippery adjustable loop.

My favourite method for setting up guy lines on a tarp or shelter, it facilitates quick removal by pulling on the working end. Tie to an improvised peg or convenient sapling.

Tents

In mountains, tundra or moorland regions where trees are scarce it is best to carry a hike tent. There are many excellent designs on the market; for comfort and longevity, look for one that has:

- plenty of room to live in – there's nothing worse than having to spend several days cramped in a tent in which you cannot sit up
- zips that are not heavily strained – if they are they will certainly fail when you need them the most
- No-See-Um netting – to prevent insects getting in
- good ventilation – my greatest criticism of some modern tent designs is that they often don't make enough allowance for the evaporation of condensation
- sound flooring material or an interchangeable underfloor for added protection
- large vestibule for stowage and cooking in inclement weather
- a design geared specifically to the conditions in which you'll be using it

Heated tents: In forests, on canoe trips or used as a base camp transported by pack animal, dog sled, four-by-four or snow mobile, no tent provides greater cheer than a heated one. My favourite is the tepee-style tent of northern Europe, now available in portable models with one central collapsible pole. These tents are a popular choice in the sub-Arctic and keep you warm and dry in the worst weather, so they are ideal for the British climate – a perfect headquarters for a youth-group expedition, for example.

Depending on the size and specifications, they can be heated either by a portable wood-burning stove, with a chimney to carry away the smoke, or a fire in a readily available collapsible firebox to prevent scorching of the ground.

Evenk tent, central Siberia.

CORDAGE

String or cordage is one of the most important resources we can carry with us into the wilderness. With it we can improvise items for use in the camp, negotiate obstacles, such as rivers or cliffs, make temporary repairs to equipment and, should the need arise, catch food.

As with so many items of our modern equipment we take for granted the presence of strong nylon cord. But in the study of bushcraft we must learn how to provide cordage for ourselves from nature. Fortunately there are many fibres to be found in the natural environment which we can utilise to make all sorts of cordage from small lines to strong ropes.

Of course, only half the story is about making cordage: it is just as important to know what to do with it once you have it. Although many believe that knots are difficult to learn, for the most part the opposite is true – particularly the ones we use in bushcraft.

IMPROVISED CORDAGE

Roots

The roots of many trees can be used to make cordage – spruce, cedar, hemlock, yew, larch and pine are particularly adaptable, but some deciduous trees, such as birch, can also be used.

The roots that you need are the long, surface ones, which are thin and flexible, found just a few centimetres beneath the ground. Generally, the best are to be found in mossy conditions where the soil is easily removed from a large area to expose them. Then they can be separated from each other and harvested. Failing this, take a short, finger-thick stick about 20cm long, and gently scrape at the ground at 90° to the direction from which you think a root might radiate out from the tree. Eventually the tip will trip over a root. Once you have found your root, excavate along its whole length – never try to pull the root from the ground as it is much more firmly attached than you may imagine and will snap; instead, be patient and take your time to unearth it. Choose a root slightly thicker than its intended purpose to allow for the relatively thick bark on the root. Take only one or two roots from each tree and carefully replace the soil. That way you will harvest a resource that

Roots can be a strong and easily available material, particularly in coniferous forests.

nature is willing to supply, and do no lasting damage within the forest.

Now prepare the root for use. First remove the bark: this is best done with a tool called a brake. To make one take a dead piece of wood that can still be split. Carve the stick like a screwdriver, cutting a V in the flat blade end about 4cm deep. Insert the root into the split and support the stick in your closed hand. Pull the root through the split and the bark will split and peel off. The root can now be dried and stored for use later in the year or be pressed into service straight away.

If you're lashing together a shelter ridgepole you need not remove the bark: choose a root strong and long enough and use it as it is. If, however, you are lacing or lashing together something that must stay tightly bound, allow the root to dry first: when it is green it will shrink considerably as it dries; if you make a lashing with it green, when the root shrinks the binding will come loose. When you use a dry root moisten it before use to make it more flexible. Traditionally, some roots, particularly those of the spruce, are improved by boiling; this increases the root's flexibility and makes it less prone to becoming brittle when dry.

You can split roots many times to make finer binding materials, and semicircular or flat binding strips that become attractive, strong and functional lashings. In northern Europe fine roots have been used to weave intricate baskets.

Withies

Withies are the wire of the woods, made from thin, flexible birch, hazel, ash, and willow wands. In our rural past, withies were used to bind together faggots of firewood for transportation to bakeries in cities, to hold in place the staves of barrels and lash together frameworks of rustic poles. You will find them most useful in the construction of shelters, campsites and all manner of backwoods projects. They have even been used to make ropes for crossing rivers. In the archaeological record, withies have been found attached to heavy objects for hauling, and lashing together the planks of early rafts.

Withies can be made in winter, but you will find it easier in the summer when the sap is well up in the tree and the fibres are most flexible. First, search for a suitable wand – it should be a young shooting sapling or branch. Choose one that is flexible, long enough for its intended purpose, and which is free of strong branching stems. Begin by stretching the wand and trimming off any side branches about 4mm from the main shoot. Next, grasping the wand and close to where it is attached to the parent tree, twist it until you hear the fibres pop. Now continue to twist gently, moving your hands towards the tip of the shoot. Hold the tip and bend the wand into an S shape rather like pedals and cranks on a bicycle. Turn the pedals carefully, which loosens the fibres, gradually working your way towards the base. Don't over-twist it or the fibres will fray and break. Almost inevitably in some places they will be less willing to loosen; at these spots you can encourage the twisting by stretching the withy and working it gently between your hands. Once you have softened the withy to its full length, you can cut it cleanly from the tree.

You can use it as it is, or split it in half to lash together poles or bundles of materials. Withies are remarkably strong and enduring, and can even be tied together with conventional knots, particularly the fisherman's knot (see page 157). I have used withies regularly to establish a rustic camp, lashing together ridgepoles, or support poles for kitchen utensils and implements. The lashings last a year easily and sometimes two before they have to be replaced.

Withies can also be re-used: in the eighteenth century bakers who received faggots of hornbeam bound with withies from woodland outside London sent the withies back to the woods for recycling. If they dry out, soaking will restore their flexibility.

In deciduous forests withies have boundless uses.

Bark

The cambium or inner bark of some trees can be removed and processed into wide sheets or thin strips of fibre. Although I shall describe how to do this with the trees to be found in the northern temperate zone, the same techniques can be applied to a wide range of trees found in other parts of the world.

Willow bark

The willow is widespread in the northern temperate zone, favouring wetland habitats. Its bark is easily removed between March and July. If you are going to use it for binding or lashing, you need only remove suitable strips and leave on the outer bark. I tend to take it from saplings 4–6cm in diameter; they provide a strong, thick bark which when cut into 5mm–1cm wide strips, produces an excellent binding material. For finer work remove the outer bark from the willow, or the inner bark will dry and become brittle. For weaving or making string, you will need a thinner, more flexible inner bark, found on saplings of an even smaller diameter.

The best place to look for suitable saplings or thick wands is in wet areas at woodland edges or along the banks of streams and small

Scrape away green outer bark.

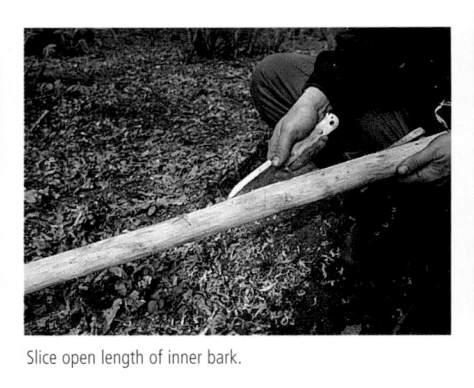

Slice open length of inner bark.

Peel bark halfway off.

Lift out wood from bark.

With care you will have a sheet of bark that can be split down to desired widths.

Save the outer bark: boil it in water with ash and bark fibres to increase the fibre's durability.

rivers. I try to find a willow tree that has fallen over with side shoots rising vertically from the trunk. Choose a straight sapling 3cm in diameter, with as few side branches as possible. Prune it carefully, using a folding saw; in this way the tree is not damaged. Next, trim off the top of the sapling and plant it in the ground, where, because of the willow's tenacious nature, it may take root and grow into a new tree.

Scrape off the dark green outer bark with the back of your knife blade. Keep the bark scrapings. Now slit the bark all the way along the sapling, then peel it half-way off the stick on either side of the split, then lift it free. It can be used straight away to tie undemanding lashings, but for more prolonged use, or for the manufacture of fine cordage, you will need to process it. Cut the inner bark into useful-sized strips, then put it into a pot with some wood ash and the saved outer bark scrapings. Simmer it for at least 40 minutes; by this time the bark will have changed colour to a deep ruddy brown. It is now more durable and flexible. Willow-bark strips can be woven into multi-coloured straps by mixing unprocessed with processed strips twisted into two or more ply cordage.

Although in theory it is impossible to remove the inner bark from the willow during winter, I have found that by using a knife to strip off the fibres it is possible to collect thin strips 20–30cm long by 4mm wide. The fibres from winter-stripped bark are stronger, making them the best choice for thin strong cord.

Lime bark

The inner bark from the lime tree was once one of the most important sources of natural cordage.

Lime trees reproduce well by suckering – that is, producing new saplings from the base of the mature tree – and suckers 5–15cm in diameter can be felled with no fear of damaging the mature tree. To remove the bark

Place long sheet of bark in slow stream.

After a month the bark smells terrible but has softened.

Now fibres can be easily split down as necessary, rinsed and dried.

from a sucker, split it the full length and pull it off like a jacket. Save the wood to season and carve: soft and light-coloured, it is a delightful wood to work with. Straight from the tree lime bark is stiff and incredibly inflexible, like plastic guttering, and seems the most unlikely material to turn into flexible cord. For quick makeshift cordage, a few fibres can be peeled away from the inside of the bark jacket. For the best cordage, though, the bark must be soaked in water for several weeks – a slow-flowing stream is ideal. After soaking it takes on a strong smell of vegetative decay and tannin which can be quite overpowering, but the layers of bark will separate freely and you can strip out large quantities of broad fibres. Wash them in fresh water to get rid of the strong smell and then hang them out to dry. In the past these were used to make strong rope, and are well suited for use in fishing lines, string, and strong cords. They can also be used for weaving.

Other barks

Many other trees yield fibre from their inner bark, including wych elm, oak and sweet chestnut. Once you're familiar with the processes by which lime and willow bark can be treated, you can adapt them to other trees. Sweet chestnut and oak inner barks can be stripped from the partially rotting bark found on fallen timbers. When dried, they make wonderfully soft flexible string.

Plant fibres

Many hundreds of plants around the world will provide you with fibres. Once you have become familiar with the ones available in your homeland you quickly learn to adapt the techniques for extracting them to strange plants in other countries.

Yucca (Yucca sp.)

Take fresh green leaves and begin by battering the sharp point at the leaf tip against a rock.

Turn the leaf round and beat the basal end, where it attaches to the main stem, against a rock to soften it. Then take the leaf in the centre between your teeth and pull downwards with your hands until the leaf is halved. Repeat the process to quarter it. These strips of leaf fibre can be knotted together base end to base end, pointy end to pointy end, and with a simple reef or square knot. In this way you can produce several metres of just the right sort of cordage for a wicking (see page 122).

Agave (Agave sp.)

The tip of the agave leaf has a hard sharp spike, which can be left attached to the fibres of the agave leaf for use as a needle. When green leaves are thick, fleshy, and cactus-like in texture soak them until the fibres pull off easily, or scrape them free, the more usual method. A word of caution here: the leaf juice may cause severe skin irritation unless it is washed off immediately after contact.

Begin by cutting a fleshy leaf with a good point low at the base of the plant – take care because the edge is covered with many tiny thorns – then slice off the edge. Next use a sharpened piece of wood or perhaps the back of your knife to scrape the flesh off the leaf – sometimes it helps to pound it a little first. Soon you see the fibres starting to free themselves. You can speed up the process by rubbing them round a nearby branch. When clean of flesh, the fibres are extremely strong and remain attached to the sharp point of the leaf. These natural 'needles and thread' were carried by Apache warriors and were strong enough to repair a damaged moccasin. Remove the sharp point to use the fibres as strong cord or string.

Wild sisal, mother-in-law's tongue (Sansevieria aethiopica)

Wild sisal is found in Africa and grows well in extremely arid conditions. It is easily

Tie the leaf strips together into long cord.

Long cord, strips and whole leaves from yucca.

Bash the base of the leaf against a rock to soften it.

From the middle of the leaf strip down the fibres four or more times.

Pull off green yucca leaf.

Blunt the sharp point on a rock.

How to produce cordage from yucca leaves

San bushman stripping pulp from fibres of *Sansevieria aethiopica*.

Stinging nettle (*Urtica sp.*)

Willowherb (*Epilobium sp.*)

recognised as it looks like pieces of green rubber hose-pipe standing upright in the ground. It is used by Bushmen in the Kalahari to produce string strong enough to snare deer or birds. A long sisal plant is cut low down, pounded with the blunt end of a digging stick, then scraped of its thick pulp with the sharp end and until the strong internal fibres have been freed.

Stinging nettle (*Urtica sp.*)
Stinging nettle produces inferior cordage but it is adequate for short-term needs. First, select tall nettles: they are best collected late in their growing season just before they begin to dry and rot. Avoid being stung; if you do not have gloves with you, use a pair of socks to protect your hands or coat your hands heavily with mud. Remove the leaves, flatten the stems gently either by squeezing them between your index finger and thumb or, if they are strong and resistant, by rolling a small stick over them on a log. Now bend the nettle in the middle to break the strong, fibrous pith inside. Remove the pith, leaving the fibres attached to the outer bark, then peel the bark into four

lengths. The fibres can be used as they are for many jobs – for example, tying a fish to a stick for cooking – or can be made up into strong cord. The finest nettle cordage is produced by drying the fibres then dampening them slightly before laying into string.

Willowherb (*Epilobium sp.*)
Willowherb can be used in the winter to provide fibres when many other fibre-producing plants are no longer available. It is the outer fibres on the stem of great willowherb, *Epilobium hirsutum*, that are used for cordage. The plant can often be found in large stands beside ponds, ditches and damp ground. It is quite easy to remove the fibres as there are no stings or acrid juices to contend with. Rosebay Willowherb *Epilobium angustifolium* (above) may also be used.

Take a dry stem and pull off any leaf stalks then gently crush the stem as you would with stinging nettles. Open the stem flat and you will find that the pith is woody; to remove it snap it every 8cm along the full length of the stem, then lift out each section of woody pith from the fibrous outer bark. The fibres need no further processing as they are usually dry already. They can be laid into cordage strong enough to make a snare or fishing line. Other plants that can be used in a similar way include evening primrose, milkweed, Indian hemp and dogbane.

Lianas

One of the best cordage resources found in the tropical rainforests. Hanging like pieces of telephone cable from the highest branches, lianas trail down towards the ground. Little needs to be done to make these fibres ready for use other than to tug carefully on the end so that they slap high up. Be careful not to pull too hard and bring down dead branches on top of your head. Also, don't look up: liana is elastic and can snap like a bungee cord.

Lianas can be found in many diameters from 3mm to 20mm; they have been used to tie bundles of leaves, for construction purposes, and even to make improvised rope bridges across fast-flowing rivers or deep chasms. When using them, watch out for the sap; if you get it on your hands don't rub your eyes or the tender parts of your body until you have washed them thoroughly.

METHODS FOR MAKING CORDAGE
The 2 ply pygmy roll (right)

1. Begin by tying together two strands of cordage fibres. These are held together with one hand (here using the left hand) while the other hand effects the twisting. Hold the strands where they meet and, using the thumb and middle finger of your free hand, roll the two strands simultaneously in the same direction until they are tightly twisted, being sure to keep them apart so that they twist independently.

2. At the end of the roll, clamp the two strands between thumb and middle finger.

Lianas

Handling cordage

Although today's ropes are generally lighter and stronger than the ropes of yesteryear, they may be more susceptible to some forms of damage than the natural ropes used in the past. For example, climbing ropes left in the boot of a car in hot weather may be severely weakened by exposure to high temperatures. Here are some rope rules.

- *Know the history of your rope: never lend any rope which you use in a life-preserving role.*

- Familiarise yourself with the manufacturer's recommendations: most reputable rope-manufacturing companies can supply you with all the relevant information you will need to care for and maintain your rope.

- Don't carry a rope when it has exceeded its recommended life.

- Handle your rope with care: many professional mountaineers insist on coiling their own rope, as others' poor technique can damage it.

- Don't tread on your rope: this forces dirt into the weave of the rope, which will abrade the fibres and weaken it.

- Don't let your rope come into contact with chemicals, which may affect its strength.

- Don't pass a rope over a sharp edge or a rough surface: pad the rope where it passes over rock with a rucksack or item of clothing. Alternatively, use a strop or sling and a karabiner to reposition the rope's passing point away from the abrasive edge.

- Small-diameter rope can become more tangled than larger rope: learn to hank your cord and avoid this. It will save you many hours of frustration.

Release the left hand and the strands will twist together as cord. Repeat the process until you have the necessary length of cordage. As the fibres in the strand start to run out twist in new fibres to each strand. Strive to maintain an even thickness in each strand.

The rope lay

For larger cords a similar process can be adopted. Clamp the point where the strands meet with your thumb. Clamp the lower twisted strand between the index and middle fingers of the left hand and hold the upper strand at the end of rolling. Releasing the thumb allows the cord to twist together.

3-strand flat plait

8-strand flat plait

① ②

4-strand round plait

① ② ③

④ ⑤ ⑥

Lap coiling: a method kind to rope,
popular for coiling climbing ropes as it
does not kink the rope.

Securing the coil.

How to coil ropes

Rope terminology

1. Working End
2. Bight
3. Loop or a single turn
4. Twist
5. Two round turns
6. Standing part
7. Standing end

Chaining a rope.

Chaining (right): chaining is useful for canoe lines as it prevents tangles, particularly in capsizes.

① ② ③

Alpine Coiling

① ② ③

④

Securing the coil.

KNOTS

In an ideal world one knot would be used for every purpose, but this isn't an ideal world and we need to be able to tie the different knots for different purposes. For instance, you may have to moor a boat, cross a river, set up a camp, and abseil down a cliff all in one journey; knowledge of a wide variety of knotting techniques will get you past these hurdles.

The overhand knot and its useful relatives
Probably the simplest of all knots, and fortunately it is incorporated in many others used in the bushcraft world, all of which are easily tied and relatively secure. The drawback of the overhand knot is that once tightened under load it can be hard to untie; use it with small-diameter cordage rather than ropes.

The overhand knot.
Used as a stopper to prevent a cord slipping through an eyelet or to prevent the sealed end of a cord fraying.

Above: Tied in doubled cord to provide a secure loop.

Right: Two-strand overhand knot. A common and effective way to tie off drawcords.

Hanking: keeping lengths of cord tidy is an everyday chore. This technique prevents tangles.

How to hank cordage

Double frost knot.
For joining climbing tapes.

④

③

②

①

Overhand bend.
A moderately secure way to join ropes and cord.

②

①

Slip knot.
The slip knot is the basis for several other useful knots.

Slip knot secured with a half hitch.

Bow string knot.
Securing a slip knot with an overhand knot as a stopper, this knot is used for bow strings by many indigenous societies.

① ②

Honda knot.
This knot was used to form the loop in a cowboy lariat as it forms a round open eye.

Fisherman's eye knot.
A slip knot secured with an overhand part forms a strong eye.

Overhand bend or fisherman's knot.
Two sliding overhand knots form a join between cords.

① ②

Double fisherman's knot.
More secure than the overhand bend, this knot has been used widely in mountaineering to join ropes and make strops.

(3)

Evenk overhand hitch.
In Siberia, nomadic reindeer-herders employ quickly-tied release knots to minimise the time their fingers are exposed to the cold. These knots are very useful.

(2)

(1)

(2)

Mooring line hitch (right).
A knot widely used for temporarily mooring small boats, which releases when the working end is pulled.

(1)

Slippery hitch (above).
A useful knot for suspending items like stuff sacks from a branch or a taut line.

The jam knot.
The jam knot is a simple lashing, which provides strength fo. a minimal expenditure of cordage. It is intended for tying in nylon cord.

Pull very tight.

The figure-eight knot and its useful relatives

The figure-eight knot — or, as it is sometimes called, the Flemish knot — is a more reliable knot than the overhand knot in that it is both secure and easily untied after loading. The figure-eight family of knots are among the most important used in the outdoors because of their widespread adoption by climbers and mountaineers. If the figure-eight knot is tied wrongly an overhand version is the result. This may be difficult to untie but will hold under strain. Use it in much the same circumstances as you would the overhand knot.

The figure-of-eight knot.
Similar to the overhand, the figure-of-eight knot is less prone to jam tight. If tied incorrectly you end up with an overhand knot which is secure, hence the figure-of-eight's popularity amongst climbers.

The figure-of-eight loop.
The most popular knot for tying into climbing harnesses and belays, the figure-of-eight is a very important knot.

The figure-of-eight bend.
A secure method of joining ropes.

The double figure-of-eight knot.
This knot provides two non-slip loops and can be used to improvise emergency climbing harnesses.

The triple figure-of-eight knot.
This knot produces three non-slip loops –
excellent for an improvised harness for
lowering, with one long loop around the
back and shoulder and two smaller leg
loops.

The bowline knot and its useful relatives

The bowline is one of the most widely employed of all knots, used to form a secure loop at the end of a rope. In mountaineering and climbing it has been superseded largely by the figure–eight, although it is still widely used in alpine mountaineering and at sea. Because of its strength, reliability and speed of tying, it is a knot with which we should all be familiar.

The bowline.
A secure, quickly-tied knot with a non-slip loop, the bowline remains popular amongst mariners and mountaineers.

The triple bowline.
Tied with doubled cordage, a triple bowline is formed with three non-slip loops. This can be used to improvise a harness for lowering.

The clove hitch and its useful relatives

Another widely used knot, easy to tie, untie, adjust and to learn because of its clear symmetry. It is an essential knot to be familiar with. The constrictor knot is a modification of the clove hitch: its exceptional security makes it one of the most useful of all knots.

The clove hitch.
Used to attach a line to a post or rail, this is a secure fastening so long as the strain comes from 90° to the post.

The buntline hitch.
With the end of this hitch constrained within the loop of the hitch, this knot does not work loose. Consequently it is a good knot for tarps and tents, remaining secure even when they are flapping in strong winds.

Round turn and two half hitches.
This knot can be tied under strain and forms a strong attachment. Take a round turn around post or beam and pass two half hitches around the standing part.

Clove hitch (tied in the bight).

The anchor bend or fisherman's bend.
This cannot be tied under strain but with the first half hitch tucked through, the round turn forms a very secure attachment.

Slippery clove hitch.
A useful knot for temporary fixing, which is easily released. It can be used to guy out to saplings.

The constrictor knot (tied with an end).
A modified clove hitch, the constrictor knot binds tightly upon itself and does not work loose.

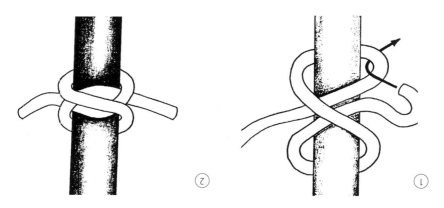

The constrictor knot (tied in the bight).

Other useful knots

(1)

The sheet bend.
The sheet bend is a quick way to join two cords – very effective if they are of differing thicknesses. It can also be used to attach cords to the corners of a sheet of material which has no eyelets. To do this, twist the corner until it can be doubled back, forming a bight through which to sheet-bend the guy.

The double sheet bend.
A more secure form of the sheet bend.

Modified or hauling sheet bend.
In this knot the working end is tucked away, streamlining the knot for hauling.

The timber hitch.

Elegant and simple, this hitch is a secure and economical method to begin lashings and taut lines. It is particularly useful tied in natural cordage.

The plank sling.

The plank sling is more easily learned when it is tied as shown here. This knot is a first-rate binding for a bundle of tent poles or sticks. Pull the sticks tight and tie off the ends.

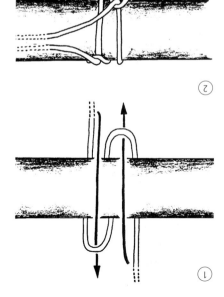

②

①

The highwayman's hitch.

A secure hitch which will release cleanly and quickly.

②

①

The lark's foot hitch.

Simple and widely used, it should not be relied upon in rescue situations with man-made fibres — under load they can heat up and melt through.

The alpine butterfly knot.
This is a non-slip knot of strength, used to tie a loop in the middle of a rope – a traditional middleman knot in mountaineering. Use it when loops are needed in a line.

The waggoner's hitch.
A simple and effective means of tensioning a rope.

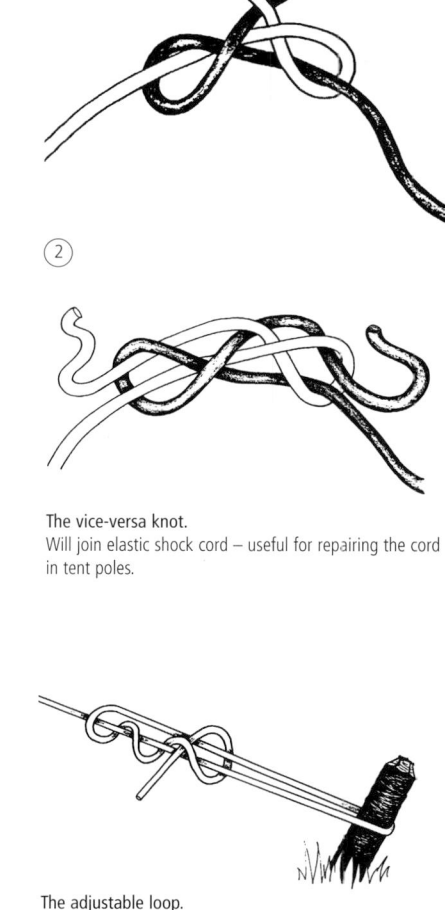

① ②

The vice-versa knot.
Will join elastic shock cord – useful for repairing the cord in tent poles.

This is better still.

The adjustable loop.
Quick and easy to tie, this knot is perfect for adjustable guylines.

It can be improved by pinning here with a stout bar.

The blood knot with inward coil.
A secure and easily tied knot for joining fishing line. When tying monofilament, wet the knot before making tight to ensure proper tightening.

The surgeon's knot.
Used to tie off sutures, the surgeon's knot will secure the ends of nylon cord where other more conventional knots – such as the reef knot – will loosen and come apart.

The first coil provides the weight and sufficient cord to reach from the branch down to the ground.

The second coil provides sufficient rope to reach from the ground to the branch.

The half blood knot.
A quick and easy knot for attaching a hook to fishing line. Wet the line before tightening.

The tree-surgeon's throwing coil (right).
This technique is used by tree surgeons to cast a rope over high branches with ease, without tangles and jams.

HITTING THE TRAIL

Throughout the planning of your journey it may seem as though setting out is the smallest part of the whole endeavour and in many ways that is true. But when you do, it is important that you are working both physically and mentally at 100 per cent. Leave behind any mental baggage that may distract you.

MENTAL PREPARATION

The moment the door shuts behind me I switch into an expedition frame of mind, and so should you. From that point forward you must pay proper attention to all the details of the journey, run over the details so that you are completely *au fait* with the minutiae. You must become active and sharp, spotting signs in the airport ahead of others, and thereby preparing yourself for the kind of alertness that makes the difference when you are in the bush. You must become willing to adapt to new circumstances and bend with the flow of the journey, like the proverbial tree on the mountain.

- Push aside any fears you may harbour so that they don't cloud your judgement at times of crisis.
- Become considerate to others around you, suppressing your own idiosyncrasies in the interests of team morale.
- Exercise your ability to think quickly and responsively; stay alert to your location and the details of your expedition so that you remain totally involved.
- Be prepared to respond to whatever circumstances you meet.
- Take a pride in negotiating challenges and obstacles and be prepared always to respond with physical as well as mental energy. It may be that you will need to be actively aggressive to solve some problems.
- Watch out for times when your mental focus slips: be prepared to tighten the nut when you are tired.
- Taking care of expedition chores yourself should be your first priority: only when you have taken care of everything should you attend to your own kit, relax and rest.
- Expect the unexpected: things inevitably go wrong when you are on the trail, but when they do, don't complain – do something about it.
- When you are working with local guides do not assume that they will be of the highest calibre: on several occasions I have been surprised by the incompetence of guides who came bearing the highest recommendations. The important thing is to be responsible for your own safety. Do not be too willing to abdicate such responsibility to others.
- If you are acting as guide, be receptive to the history and experience of other members of your party: they may be highly competent, yet in the early stages of an expedition seem not to be so because they are adapting and acclimatising to new environmental challenges. Orientation is a key early phase of any expedition.
- Switch on your memory: make certain you know what items of equipment you have with you, where you put them last and what you used them for so that you don't lose anything. The simpler your outfit, the easier it is to maintain.
- Stay alert to possible threats: you may be travelling through an area where you are at risk of theft, so don't make yourself a target.
- Lastly, develop empathy with your environment: allow nature into your life while you are on the trail. Make the most of enjoying your surroundings. After all, that is why you are there.

SETTING THE PACE

When we are walking in the back country we will most likely be carrying rucksacks loaded with a considerable amount of equipment, food and clothing; we will be unable to walk as freely as we would unburdened in a city street. It is easy in the bush to find ourselves tiring, twisting ankles and ending up with blisters on our feet. If you are new to walking with a rucksack and boots, bear in mind while you are planning the journey that you must condition yourself to this. Get used to wearing a rucksack with a load in it and learn to walk efficiently for long periods without injuring yourself: move at a steady pace, taking care not to twist an ankle or to shift your feet unnecessarily within your boots, acquiring blisters.

One of the most important things about walking with a rucksack is to establish a comfortable pace: a good guide is your heartbeat. Try to find a speed at which you are not exerting yourself on the level. As you move uphill, shorten your stride and reduce your speed to maintain an even heart-rate. Although at first this may seem slow and uncomfortable, in the long run those who keep the steadiest pace tend to travel further for the expenditure of fewer calories. It's a good idea to stop every hour and rest for a few moments – anyone who has a sore spot on a foot can take off their boot and apply some moleskin to prevent rubbing. You can also check your navigation, then update everyone on where you are going. Frequent breaks enable the party leader to maintain proper communication with the group. Don't stop for too long, though: your body will cool and when you start again you will be stiff and more prone to muscular injuries.

Perhaps it is in the high mountains where you really see the advantage of maintaining a steady pace. Alpine mountaineers learn to move at an almost painfully slow pace: they plod along, moving only a few inches at each step, contending not only with the load on their back and the snow under their feet but also with the thin air of the Alpine environment.

With experience the pace will quicken and a party of experienced hikers will be able to move swiftly all day. But in a group of mixed ability the pace must be set to suit the slowest person.

In cold conditions when you stop on the trail you will probably need to put on a garment to keep you warm. It is a good idea to keep this to hand at the top of your rucksack. When you first stop you are initially still warm from the hiking but it takes only a few moments, especially in a breeze, to become chilled.

CARING FOR YOUR FEET

At the end of a hard day's walking, take off your boots. Leave your socks on for a few extra moments to allow your body heat to drive out some of their accumulated moisture, but then take them off, turn them inside out and air them. Now attend to your feet. If you have enough time, wash them with soap and water so they do not build up bacteria that can cause problems like athlete's foot. Allow them to dry, and as they are drying, massage them. This is important if they have been damp all day or if they have been cold: a

massage will help to revitalise them. Dust them with foot powder. If you do this every day or even every other day, your feet will stay in good shape.

Now for fresh socks, and if you have with you some lightweight shoes, put them on and leave your boots to air. Take very good care of your socks: try not to drop them into grit, sand or pine needles, which may get into the weave of the sock and later cause a blister.

Blisters

The bane of all foot travellers, they can be painful and debilitating. Once established they last for several days and are difficult to cure. If you detect a hot spot developing within your boot, stop immediately and do something about it.

The way to treat a hot spot is to apply some moleskin or mole foam, which provides padding and reduces friction between your foot and your boot. If necessary you can cut out a ring bandage from the mole foam so that the boot is held away from the tender spot on your foot.

Advice with regard to the treatment of blisters varies enormously, but this works for me.

First, assess the position of the blister. If it is on a part of your foot that is likely to be continuously rubbed, like your heel or the ball of your foot, you will need to drain it then pad and dress it. Wash your foot carefully. If this is not possible use an antiseptic wipe from your medical kit around the area of the blister. Then take a needle from your first-aid kit and your lighter. Heat the needle to sterilise it, and when it is cool, carefully pierce the blister bubble close to its edge and gently squeeze out the fluid. Apply a topical antiseptic to the spot where it has been drained then dress the blister with a non-adhesive dressing. This may provide sufficient padding but, if not, apply a small strip of mole foam over the top.

If the blister has burst, you must prevent it becoming infected. It must be kept clean, and if necessary apply some topical antiseptic in the early stages of treatment. Cover the blister with a non-adhesive dressing then pad it carefully to prevent further abrasion or rubbing. Hydrocolloid dressings are excellent for treating such blisters. If you are carrying an antibacterial ointment use some to facilitate rapid healing – I have had great success with Flamazine.

Toenails
Nails should be kept short. An in-growing toenail may hinder your progress. An old method of dealing with it is to scrape the top of the nail with the edge of your knife, a file, a piece of emery paper or even a roughened rock like a pumice stone until it can be easily depressed in the middle by your thumbnail. The pressure on the in-growing part of the nail is lessened and your foot will be more comfortable.

Sprained ankles
Perhaps the most common walking injury, a severely sprained ankle often resembles a fracture, causing lameness, swelling and pain, and may mean two or three days' rest on the trail. Try to avoid ankle injuries: cut a staff when you are traversing steep, slippery slopes for extra support.

If you do sprain your ankle, remember the old medical treatment RICE: it stands for Rest; Ice or cold compress treatment to reduce the swelling; a Compressive bandage – use the cohesive bandage from your medical kit (see page 16); and Elevation of the limb to help reduce inflammation. If you take off your boot straight away with such an injury you may find it impossible to get it back on because your foot has swollen. It may be more appropriate to continue moving with your boot on until you reach a safer and more appropriate place to stop and examine the injury.

Bandaging an ankle.

Trench foot

Non-freezing cold injuries are associated with backcountry travel after prolonged exposure to moderate or severe cold when the weather is damp and the ground sodden. If your feet have been consistently wet for three days or thereabouts, you are likely to develop trench foot. In severe cases the toes or foot may swell and even blister. Trench foot is serious and the casualty should be taken to hospital.

To prevent it, dry your feet properly at the end of each day, warm them and massage them. Non-freezing cold injuries are more prevalent in people who are undernourished and dehydrated: make sure you eat and drink enough.

At –48°C, to prevent frostbite, students in the arctic learn to rewarm cold feet on the stomach of a team mate. Clothing removed (note glove) should be stuffed inside other clothing, not left to freeze on the ground.

Frostbite

Frostbite occurs in temperatures below freezing when the tissues of your foot have frozen. It is usually associated with either footwear which is too tight or where your whole body has become chilled: due to vaso-constriction insufficient blood supply to the extremities has resulted in their freezing. When the thermometer reads –30 degrees Centigrade or below we cannot afford to make a mistake in terms of the care of our feet.

If you find that your foot is becoming cold you can help to rewarm it by shaking it, and the same is true of your hands to increase the blood supply to these. If that fails to work then you must consider asking your teammate to rewarm your foot under his armpit next to his skin, skin-to-skin contact, making sure that you keep your boot off the ground where it will not freeze solid. If you are standing around a lot in very cold conditions put insulation between your feet and the ground. Use spruce boughs or any other such material.

If your foot does freeze you will find that your toes become white and waxy; you must then consider how seriously frostbitten they are. Minor frostbite is only superficial and can be rewarmed effectively, but deep tissue frostbite where your foot or toes are solidly frozen is more serious. With serious frostbite it is better to continue travelling with your foot frozen but try to prevent any deepening of the freezing rather than thawing it, which is painful, leading to swelling and usually blisters.

If you have frostbitten feet you will need to seek medical assistance. Under no circumstances should you attempt amputation. Today hospital treatment allows the foot to regenerate and heal gradually, protecting it from infection with antibiotics

Drying socks and boots

As damp footwear can cause serious problems, consider carefully how you will dry it. If you take with you some waterproof socks, you will always be able to keep your feet dry even if your boots are wet. However, at the end of a day's hiking you should still dry your footwear as best you can. Don't place your boots too close to a fire: the leather will dry out, shrink and crack. Dry your boots slowly with the opening upward. Today if you are in a cabin, you may be able to stuff them with newspaper.

In the bush open your boots as wide as possible, scrub away dirt from the outside and

When using a tarp, set your boots on sticks to prevent them filling with rain.

leave them in a dry, shady place, off the ground.

In cold weather take them into your sleeping-bag at night to prevent them freezing solid: place them in the sleeping-bag stuff sack first to keep yourself and your sleeping-bag dry. At the end of a trip clean and reproof your boots with Nikwax aqueous wax. Store them in a cool, dry place.

WATER OBSTACLES
Water is a powerful natural force in the landscape. Whenever you cross it, pay attention to safety. Drowning accounts for a large number of backcountry deaths – and it is often experienced swimmers who drown.

Water in the wild presents a different set of problems from that of a swimming pool. For a start it may be moving, and although seemingly moving slowly actually moving with immense force. Water in wild areas is often very cold, perhaps even fed by glacial melt waters: if you fall in the shock will make you gasp and thereby inhale water. Also water may obscure obstacles on the riverbed. When travelling in wild areas avoid directly crossing a water hazard. If this is not possible search for the easiest way of crossing.

River crossing
In wild areas, rivers and other waterways are an essential means of travel for canoeists and even walkers. In rainforests they are a vital navigational aid. As you travel further into the wilderness, bridges, cables or basket crossings are few and far between. Sometimes there may be no alternative but to cross a river as it may be too large to hike round. Remember that after heavy rainfall even small streams turn into raging torrents, and that the force of water must never be underestimated. Train yourself to deal with it.

Risks
Whenever we cross a river we are at risk from the debris being carried within the river, such as trees and branches; in really strong currents, even rocks and giant boulders can be moved along. Sometimes you can even hear them being moved along in the water. When this is the case we should not attempt to cross it.

But apart from its strength, perhaps the most dangerous aspect of water is the cold. Many wilderness rivers are fed from glacial melt waters and mountain streams and the temperature may only be a few degrees above freezing point. Certainly more than cold enough to cause us serious problems. It is not uncommon for travellers in the bush to attempt to cross a river, only to decide that the water is too cold to cross at that point, then search for a narrower point to cross. Whenever we enter cold water our body suffers cold shock (see above, water obstacles) which may make it difficult for us to exit the water at the far bank.

There are other dangers associated with water: of being swept away by a strong current, bashed against branches and held against the current, whirlpools, an ankle trapped between rocks.

Perhaps the most dangerous thing of all is overconfidence. Whenever we are involved in crossing water we must pay the greatest attention to safety procedures and plan our crossing with great care.

Crossing water

When confronted with a water obstacle, evaluate the level of risk, decide whether the crossing is feasible, find the most suitable place to cross and organise it. Remember

W	Water
A	Assess
S	Search
P	Plan
T	Technique
A	Anticipate
R	Rewarm

Begin by considering the type of *water* that confronts you. Is it tidal? Is it cold? Is it deep or shallow? Consider any hazards that might lurk within it, particularly animals like crocodiles. Now you will know whether it is feasible or not to cross it.

If it is, assess the crossing. Look for the run-out of the river: in other words, what is downstream of where you may cross? Notice hazards, such as trees, branches or snags, either natural or man-made: swept away, you might end up hanging on these. Are there rapids or, worse, waterfalls below your current location? If so, it would be foolhardy to cross at that point. What about whirlpools? Judge the speed of the river by throwing a stick into the flow and walking along beside it. Assess the nature of the riverbed. Is it muddy? If so, you may get stuck. Are there slippery boulders that might trap a foot? Assess the depth of the water: is it deep all the way across or is there a point at which the depth is more contained? Perhaps there is a sandbar half-way. Assess the human aspect of the crossing. Are the members of your party strong swimmers? If you are going into the wild you should be able to swim. Lastly, consider any alternatives: consult your map or send someone on a scouting reconnaissance; you may discover a point further upstream where the river is braided and you can wade over through shallows from sandbar to sandbar.

Search for the ideal place to cross. Avoid crossing a stream just up from where it joins a river: the speed of the water is faster here and anyone who is swept away may end up beyond rescue. Avoid bends in the river and look for a straight section between bends to cross with a gentle bend below your crossing point. The current moves fastest on the outside of a bend so don't aim to complete your crossing here. Arrange your crossing so that the far bank is just upstream of the inside of a bend: you will find that if someone is swept away, they will be able to swim more easily in the slower-moving water or even find a safe eddy to exit from. Consider carefully your potential entry and exit points: find an easy place to enter, not a steep-sided slippery or rocky bank where someone may fall and bang their head.

Plan the river crossing. This must involve the whole team so that everyone understands what is going to happen: the order in which the team will cross, the technique to be employed and any contingency plans – you may need to take into account someone's nervousness. It is sometimes a good idea to team weaker people with stronger ones.

If you are swept off your feet, keep your head out of the water, with your feet raised and pointing downstream.

Remember that when you are dealing with a moving body of water it can be impossible to hear someone on the far side of the river or even if they are beside you.

Your technique is all important: select one that is appropriate, simple and safe. Don't incorporate rope unless this is absolutely necessary. A simple method of crossing a river, such as wading side by side, providing each other with support, is usually easier to carry through. Rehearse on dry land before you enter the water.

Anticipate problems – and ask for help in this. Here two experienced minds are always better than one. You may come up with simple things, like being unable to communicate verbally above the din of the river: be prepared to use hand signals. Have a rescue procedure in place in case anyone is swept downstream. Consider the consequences for each individual of crossing the water: after heavy rainfall river water may be full of bacteria and anyone with an open wound will need to wash it afterwards. Also, if the water is cold you must be prepared to produce hot drinks: pack kindling and timber or a stove, drink ingredients and mugs in a dry bag close to the top of the first rucksack to go across.

Rewarm after crossing, and allow at least an hour for this. You will be much colder than you anticipate, unless you are in the tropics. Make sure that everyone changes into dry clothes, then gathers together around a fire or hiking stove, and has a warming, calorie rich drink.

Dressing to cross a river

Some hikers prefer to remove most of their clothing before crossing water. However, in cold conditions it is wise to keep some on. I usually opt to wear lightweight, fast-drying spare clothing, and pack my sleeping equipment and everyday clothes carefully to stop them getting wet. When wading across a slow-flowing stream, tote your rucksack high up on your shoulders.

At other times you will have to rely on dry bags, which will make your rucksack more buoyant in water. Some suggest making your rucksack into a buoyancy aid by attaching your sleeping mat to the top and wearing both shoulder straps. I don't recommend this: there have been accidents where people have been trapped by their rucksack on a snag or between rocks and drowned. It is wiser to rely on the old-fashioned method of wearing your rucksack over one shoulder. In this way, if you fall in, you can easily let go of your rucksack. If you are strapped into it and it fills with water, it may drag and hold you under water.

While crossing water, keep with you your most important items of survival equipment: your knife and a means of starting a fire. Keep your boots on: if you cross a stream barefoot you may slip on slimy rocks, slide into the crevices between them and end up with severe bruising, twisted or fractured ankles – or, worse still, trapped. I take off my socks and, once I'm back on dry land, I put on waterproof socks between dry socks and the wet boots.

To cross shallow water

Perhaps surprisingly even the smallest brook can be a safety hazard. While most people will stride or leap across, others are less confident, especially when they are carrying a rucksack. In rainforests you can often cross streams on fallen trees, which act as natural bridges. But this requires nerve and a good sense of balance. Make sure to watch weaker members of a party and encourage them to cross boldly. Sometimes it's easier for them to sit astride the log and ease their way across; someone more confident can carry over their rucksack. If you plan to travel regularly in the rainforest it is a good idea to train yourself to walk with a rucksack across such obstacles: often the tops of these logs are slippery, especially when you're wearing boots – and the water may be six or seven metres below.

A common way for a party to cross a stream is hopping from rock to rock – natural stepping stones. However, not everyone is nimble-footed, especially if they aren't used to wearing hiking boots. Beware of slips, which may result in ankle injuries and distress from the shock of falling into water, soaked equipment and clothing. You can vault over some small rivers with a stout walking staff, a fun and efficient way to do it that ensures your feet stay dry. The staff must be strong enough to support your body weight plus your loaded rucksack. Don't attempt it with a collapsible walking staff.

Unless the current is very strong, you can wade through rivers that come up to your knees. But there are still a few things to keep in mind. Whenever you wade across a stream, face upstream so that you will see any objects being carried towards you in the water and be able to avoid them. Also if the water is deeper than you thought and you are facing upstream, the force of the water locks your knees so that you stay upright.

Take great care in placing your feet: move sideways gradually in short steps and wait until you are balanced after one step before trying to take the next – you can't walk across a stream in the same way that you would across paving stones. Don't try to hurry it.

When the water reaches above the knee, perhaps to waist height, I like to take a stout staff with me. It acts as a third leg, giving me a wider, more stable base for support. If you do this face upstream and place the staff well ahead of you, keeping your legs wide apart to create a triangular base for your body. Keep two points of support in contact with the riverbed at all times.

If there are several people in your party you can wade across a river providing each other with support. Link arms, grasp clothing or each other's rucksack straps. If there are three of you, face inwards towards each other, then take hold to form a human tripod. Another

A stout staff gives strong triangular support.

Current.

Heading.

Good support but difficult to co-ordinate.

Current.

Heading.

Excellent triangular support, excellent co-ordination. Remember to watch upstream.

method involves supporting each other as in a queue, one person behind the other. When using this method the fourth person uses a staff and faces upstream.

To cross deep water

When crossing deeper water you won't be able to remain in contact with the riverbed, so consider making flotation aids, particularly if the water is very cold.

For example, if you remove your trousers, knot them at the bottom of each leg, draw them over the top of your head to fill with air and then tuck them under your armpits they may act as water wings; or inflate your therma-rest mattress; empty your water bottles and tie them together. Or put the contents of your rucksack into a dry bag, then into a stuff sack. Wrap the whole thing in a lightweight shelter sheet to make an effective float. The last option is perhaps the most efficient of all: the Archimedes principle says that an item floats because it is lighter than the weight of the volume of water it displaces, and one rucksack so wrapped will help two people stay afloat. If you tie several together you can improvise a crude raft so that it supports your chests with your legs kicking to propel you along.

When you enter cold, deep water you will experience the cold-shock reaction. You can reduce its severity with training, for example by taking a cold shower each day before you set off. Royal Navy helicopter pilots are encouraged to do this in case they have to ditch in cold water. When you experience cold shock, keep calm, hang on to your flotation aid and stay close to the shore. After a few moments it will wear off as you get used to the water temperature. Then strike out for the opposite shore. But the cold will sap your energy: before you reach the half-way point decide whether or not you have energy left to make it all the way. Cross in pairs, if possible, and encourage each other on the way.

Trousers can be used as a buoyancy aid - knot the ends of the legs and draw them quickly over your head to fill with air. Passed under your armpits, they function as very effective water wings.

To cross a large body of slow or still water

If you have to cross a large body of slow-moving water or a lake, the water may be too cold to swim across, even with a flotation aid. Instead, you will have to improvise a boat. This can be done in a variety of ways; usually the safest and easiest is the improvised tarpaulin dinghy.

SNOW OBSTACLES

In the far north, you will probably travel by snowmobile. These machines enable you to travel great distances swiftly and are made to be reliable.

However, operating in some of the most hostile conditions on Earth, they occasionally break down and you will have to be able to walk on deep snow. Also, snowmobile travel gives you a false impression of how far you have come in walking terms. The rule is that if you travel for fifteen minutes on a snowmobile it will take you twenty-four hours without snowshoes. So always carry with you a pair of snowshoes that fit conveniently on a snowmobile – and can be used to dig a track

How to cross a large body of slow or still water

Make two oval rings of 60cm stakes.

Fill between the stakes with brushwood.

Bind around the brushwood to complete oval facine.

Remove stakes and fit deck.

Lay down tarp and grass or bracken padding.

Place facine on tarp deck-side down.

Tie tarp over facine. Improvise a paddle.

Away you go.

A very stable platform with which to reach the best fishing spots.

Tie boot in place with heel free to lift.

Method of tightening to raise tip.

Point of balance.

In higher latitudes, use small wispy branches and cord to form a snow shoe like this.

if it gets bogged down in snow – or skis. But what if you forget them? If you're in forested country, you can improvise snowshoes. They won't be as effective as the real thing, but they're better than nothing.

Navigation

The most important bushcraft skill of all. You must be able to navigate to find your way safely through remote areas. You should be familiar with the use of maps, compasses and global positioning system (GPS) in their basic operation and the techniques associated with them. Then, learn to emphasise certain aspects of those techniques: you train yourself to think in navigational terms, to recognise signs in the landscape to keep you on your path. Navigation is a holistic process: a good navigator doesn't slavishly follow map and compass. As you gain experience you will acquire the ability to correct mistakes in estimation and direction swiftly. Most important of all, when your map, compass and conventional navigation equipment fail you, you will be able to find your way.

Map work

Whenever we navigate with a map or compass, we have to work with a degree of inaccuracy: map-makers often have to compromise on position, perhaps to reduce crowding on a small-scale map. Compass accuracy depends on the movement and mechanics of the instrument. When we are navigating we must avoid introducing further inaccuracy into the equation. If you ask someone to show you on a map where you are, they normally point their finger at the area where they think they are and say, 'Here, somewhere.' That won't do. Instead they should be able to reply, 'We are 100m east of this fenced junction,' or 'You're 250m north of the river junction indicated here,' and point at the map with the corner of a compass, the tip of a knife or a pine needle. All it takes is a little practice.

A few things are worth bearing in mind here. You will normally march on a 1:50,000 or 1:25,000 scale map. If you are using a 1:50,000 scale map, 1km is represented by 2cm, therefore 1cm = 500m, 2mm = 100m, so when you are working on a 1:50,000 scale map you can estimate hundreds of metres easily. The same is true for a 1:25,000 where 1km is represented by 4cm, 500m = 2cm and 100m = 4mm.

To estimate distances travelled across land you can use a timing chart: with this you time your travel across a known distance measured from your map then relate that to the chart to find your speed. It's especially useful in open terrain, particularly when travelling at night or in poor visibility. I have one taped to the lid of my compass.

In close cover it is easier to use pacing to estimate distances covered; here you will need to establish how many steps you take to cover 100m. Count the pacing of one foot only. You will find that your pacing varies according to the ground state and your load, so will need to pace yourself over 100m in varying terrains and conditions to find an average. Some people carry a string of beads to count out the paces they take and from that work out the kilometres covered. Others use a mechanical counter. With practice you can become more accurate than a GPS (global positioning system) or at least equal to it.

Contours

The undulation of the terrain affects our ability to judge distance. In learning map-reading we are taught that the map is a two-dimensional representation of a three-dimensional land surface, and that contour lines indicate the rise and fall of a slope: the tighter together the contour lines, the steeper the ground; the wider apart, the more level. From studying contour lines, you will be able to build an accurate representation of how the going will be when you travel across the landscape. Again experience helps, and the only way to learn to relate contour lines to land surfaces is to get out on the ground with a map. There is no other way. Experience on the ground is vital in learning to navigate.

Consider buying an altimeter in the form of a wristwatch; Sunto make an excellent one. Altimeters indicate altitude accurately as long as you follow the manufacturers' instructions and re-zero it regularly at known points of altitude taken from your map: atmospheric pressure may cause it to give a false reading.

When you are working with contour lines, watch for an increase in the contour interval. Usually it is 5m but in mountainous terrain cartographers often use a 20m interval so that the lines do not become too complicated on the map. Also in some parts of the world no symbols are used to indicate a cliff face: you will see tightly packed contours of a large interval – stay alert to this and check the map's legend. In some countries it's wise to check the reliability of the local mapping: you can't always rely on it!

River direction

When travelling in wild areas it's important to know in which direction rivers flow. Work this out before you go and if you feel it will help put an arrow on the map to indicate it.

LIVING FROM THE LAND

In most survival episodes shelter, water, fire and signalling must be attended to before food needs. But when lack of food does become an issue, it becomes the key obstacle to human survival.

Foraging skills have traditionally been an important part of the outfit of wilderness professionals. If you intend to step or paddle out of the far side of a national park you will need to become acquainted with them. Bear in mind that successful foraging is not a process of ruthless exploitation, but one of respect.

CALORIES

To live we burn food as fuel to generate energy, usually measured in joules or kcal. Before we begin to collect calories we must take steps to reduce energy wastage, particularly in cold climates: clothing and shelter must be adequate or improved to provide a warm, dry calorie-trapping environment.

Every environment provides its own problems from the point of view of foraging, but perhaps the most difficult of all are those of extreme cold or damp cold, where our calorific requirement is higher and where calories are difficult to obtain, there being fewer plant sources available. As we move towards the tropics more energy-rich plant foods become available, although meat still plays an important role in a survival diet. However, there are many places where foraging may be futile – high in mountain environments or where food resources are out of season. Nomadic groups travel more by necessity than choice.

Long after the flesh of the marula fruit has rotted away the seeds can be smashed open to obtain an edible kernel.

The effects of food deprivation

The first few days without food are a critical time for anyone trying to make the step from surviving to living in the wilderness. It is in this period that we exhaust the body's store of carbohydrate.

Because carbohydrates such as starches and sugars are composed of simple, easily digested molecules, they are an efficient food source that can be digested with little waste. Quickly and easily converted to energy, carbohydrates are vital in the supply of energy to the brain and nervous system and are consequently utilised before the other food sources of fat and protein.

We store carbohydrate in the muscles, the liver and a small amount in the blood. For use this is converted to glucose then transported to wherever it is needed, particularly the brain and nervous system, by the blood. The rate at which we exhaust our store of carbohydrate depends on how hard we are working, but can be as little as three or four hours when working hard in a cold environment. When our reserve of carbohydrate is exhausted our blood-sugar level drops, resulting in a reduced supply of energy to the brain. Because the brain is unable to store energy for itself it demands a continuous supply; when there is a reduction in supply various symptoms are triggered: tiredness; headache; easy irritation; loss of concentration; reduced ability to make decisions; depression; increased susceptibility to cold; increased concern with oneself.

As time goes on, fast intensive work becomes difficult; even walking up a moderate slope seems impossible. Tasks which at other times would be straightforward, such as crossing water, now become hazardous.

Adjusting to the exhaustion of carbohydrate

When our reserves of carbohydrate have been exhausted the body mobilises fats and proteins to ensure a continuing supply of energy to the brain.

Fats are found in butter, cheese, oils, nuts, egg yolks, animal fats and vegetable oils. They are more complex foods than carbohydrates, consequently the energy in fat is more slowly released than that in carbohydrate, providing a longer lasting form of energy. This is particularly well suited to slow, monotonous work, but provides a poor source of energy for fast, intensive activity. A fat-rich diet increases the need for water. In extremely cold climates a lower carbohydrate intake (40%) and a higher fat intake should be eaten to help maintain body warmth. If we eat fat-rich food before sleeping, we sleep warmer.

Ketone toxicity

One of the by-products of carbohydrate depletion is an increase in the use of fatty acids within our muscles as our activity levels increase. Remember that fat burns in a carbohydrate flame: when we are low on carbohydrate we are unable to burn body fat efficiently. In these circumstances too large a consumption of fat results in the production of waste products called ketones, which leads to headaches, nausea, difficulty in drinking, the loss of body salts and energy.

The poisonous puff-adder may seem a threat to some; to others, it is a meal.

Ketones are excreted in the urine and breath, identified by a characteristic acetone (pear-drop) scent. If you over-exert yourself under such circumstances you may be overwhelmed by the build-up of ketones in your blood, leading to a coma similar to that experienced by a diabetic.

Protein

Proteins have the most complex molecules of any food type; this means that they are the most inefficient food for energy production. The digestive process breaks proteins down into various amino acids, which are converted into new body tissue proteins such as muscle.

Complete proteins, provide the body with the exact balance of amino acids it requires to rebuild itself; some amino acids are essential for the body to function. Examples of complete protein sources are: fish; meat;

poultry; blood. Incomplete proteins lack one or more of the amino acids: for example, cheese; milk; cereal; grains; legume seeds

Ideally a survival diet should contain 75–80g complete proteins each day.

However, if only incomplete proteins are available two or more types of food may need to be eaten in combination to provide complete protein. Grains and legume seeds eaten in combination contain all of the essential amino acids.

Because proteins are the most complex type of food they supply energy after carbohydrate and fat reserves have been used up. Lack of protein results in malnutrition, skin and hair disorders as well as muscle atrophy.

The average body contains approximately six kilograms of protein in the muscles, as a source of energy it is less important: its prime function is as the building material for cells and stomach enzymes. Without protein the body cannot repair itself, a high protein intake increases our need for water.

Minerals

Minerals (salts) are needed so the range of different chemical processes can work within the body. For example, iron binds oxygen within the blood; potassium and sodium aid nerve function; calcium is the building block of the skeleton. Problems associated with mineral deficiency are only likely to occur when you have not eaten a balanced diet over several weeks.

Vitamins

Vitamins carry out important work in different body processes. Vitamin B is involved in energy conversion; vitamin C is important in the intake of iron within the intestine, assists cells and tissues in holding together, and maintains a healthy immune system; vitamins A, D and K assist eyesight, intake of calcium and blood coagulation.

Vitamins B and C cannot be stored within the body: vitamin C is found in many plants while vitamin B is found in some plants and the liver of animals.

It is worth bearing in mind that some plants contain toxins that reduce the efficacy of vitamin B.

Fibre

Fibre aids the efficient functioning of the stomach and intestine. If eating again after a period of starvation, take only small amounts of fibre, increasing gradually.

A foraging strategy

Calories

The requirement of an average person doing an average job is approximately 3000 calories per day. Experiments show that a healthy person can subsist for a considerable period of time on 500 calories of carbohydrate a day without harmful effect. For this reason we should strive to attain this each day, bearing in mind that in colder weather, when injured, ill or working hard this will need to increase. In those circumstances, we must provide ourselves with more than 500 calories of carbohydtrate per day, and fat.

Types of food

Carbohydrate, found in plants, is easier to obtain than meat. Search first for edible plants.

If game is readily obtained it is possible to subsist indefinitely in good health on a diet of meat, fat and water.

Methods of obtaining food

Nothing ventured; nothing gained

When it comes to finding food we need to be open minded; many sources of nutrition will be strange to us, some even repugnant. But if it is a matter of survival we must not allow prejudice to deter us from obtaining nourishment. It is important to note that many of the best techniques for obtaining food in the wild are now regulated or banned. In a real emergency no one is going to quibble over the way you find food, but if you wish to travel and supplement your rations with wild food you must stay within the law, restricting yourself to the foods and techniques permissible.

Sadly, regulations are sweeping over many wild plant foods that do not need saving from foragers. As you will discover, the most important wild foods are the most common and readily available plants.

Plants

Learning to recognise edible plants is a rewarding study: even if you are no amateur botanist you can learn to identify a few important edible species.

For survival use a plant should be common, provide carbohydrate, ideally for a prolonged period of the year, be easily used without the need for complicated processing, and easily recognised. If it can be confused for a toxic species you must know how to differentiate between them. Try always to know the habitat in which a plant grows.

Bear in mind that the most energy-rich plant foods are those with edible roots, seeds (including nuts), or fruits. Of lesser survival value are the greens, which contain less nourishment but which will supply a ready source of vitamins and minerals.

Once you can correctly identify an edible plant you must also know how to process it. Plants have a wide range of defence mechanisms from thorns to a complex array of toxins that can kill quickly, cause serious dermatitis and blister the predator's mouth, interfere with the predator's ability to reproduce, or even cause slow starvation by preventing the conversion of carbohydrate to energy.

Energy equation

Almost nothing about foraging is straightforward, and it is important to maximise your return while reducing your energy expenditure. This means being able to prioritise your locally available food sources and having the right knowledge to obtain them easily. For example, roots growing in sandy soils are frequently larger than those in clay and are considerably easier to extract. Bear in mind that it may be better to collect several small roots that are easily dug up than struggle to excavate one large root from difficult soil. Bear in mind that there are techniques to maximise the collection and processing of wild foods; for example, beech nuts open when warmed by the fire, saving tedious work in splitting open the cases. Acorns can be winnowed from leaf litter or put into a slow flowing stream where they sink while the leaf litter floats away.

Roots

Cat-tail Typha spp: Provides carbohydrate at any season of the year. Cat-tail has a seed head

Cat-tail *Typha spp*

Cat-tail roots

that looks like a sausage on a stick and grows in ditches at the margins of ponds and in areas of very slow-flowing water.

Reach down underneath the plant into the ooze in which it grows and you will find rope-like rhizomes stretching sideways as a subterranean mat intertwining and interlocking with each other. If you pull these up carefully they are a creamy yellow colour with lots of small rootlets on the outside. They feel somewhat leathery and a little hollow. If you cut one through you will find a spongy layer just underneath the outer surface enclosing a tightly compressed bundle of long fibres covered in a starchy substance. This is the most important part of the plant and has a very high food value. The easiest way to use this is to harvest these roots, break them into lengths of about 30–40cm and throw them on to the embers of a fire until they are charred black all over. Remove them from the fire, break the outer surface, pull the central fibres free with your teeth and suck the starchy pulp from them, spitting the fibres out. Cooked correctly they taste like warm sweet chestnut and are delicious. They can also be eaten raw but they don't taste anywhere near as good and you may run the risk of picking up a parasite from the water.

Other parts of the Cat-tail are also edible. The young shoots or corms emerging from the base of the central flowering stem of the plant can be collected and stir-fried. The central starchy core at the base of the flowering stem, which is very hard and white, can be diced and added to stews for long slow cooking or can even be sliced thinly and deep fried to make an improvised form of potato chip. As the flowering shoot emerges from a new plant the base of the plant in the early summer and late spring can be cut free from the root and you will see that it resembles a leek, often referred to as Cossack Asparagus. The white tip to this part of the plant is frequently eaten raw or sliced and added to salads. As the flower head begins to develop you will find that, like an ear of sweetcorn, it will be encased in folded leaves and a light emerald green in colour. This provides a good mid-season snack steamed and served with butter (if available) just like corn on the cob.

The plant has quite a few other uses: the leaves can be used to improvise rope and other cordage and woven into mats for cooking and other purposes. The dried flowering stalk from the previous year makes a good hand drill, although somewhat delicate, and the seed head can be used for tinder. The seed heads can also be collected and used to stuff clothing to improvise a duvet by placing the broken open seed heads in between the lining and outer layer of a jacket.

Burdock Arctium spp*: A wonderful wild food that occurs at the edge of woodland and in disturbed open ground. It comprises a large

heart-shaped leaf with a distinctive rich, musty odour. In its second year it grows with a flowering stalk on which are spiky round seed heads that attach themselves to woollen clothing as we brush past them.

Burdock *Arctium spp*

Burdock is a biennial, which means it completes its life cycle over a period of two years.

Collect the root of the burdock from the completion of its first year's growth to the

The root of a burdock after a year's growth is swollen with starchy goodness.

Dandelion *Taraxacum officinale*

Sow Thistle *Sonchus oleraceus*

Bristly Ox Tongue *Picris echioides*

Pig Nut *Conopodium majus* – likes shady woods.

Pig Nut *Conopodium majus* – note the 90° turn in the stem.

Pig Nut *Conopodium majus*

beginning of its second year's growth. Spring roots are sweeter than autumn gathered roots and can be eaten raw, while autumn and winter gathered roots are best roasted in hot ashes or diced into stews. Roast it in the rind, but peel before stewing it. The only difficulty with collecting burdock is that it prefers to grow in hard ground.

These related plants are widespread, considered weeds. Their roots can be eaten after first scraping away the outer rind, slicing and soaking in plenty of water for an hour or more. Then add them to stews or roast as parsnips. Dandelion and Sow Thistle can be rather bitter, but the Bristly Ox Tongue is less so. They are less bitter when collected before the plant flowers.

Pig Nut Conopodium majus: Pig Nut is a true wild delicacy. Its delicate leaves can be found

Lesser Celandine *Ranunculus ficaria* in flower

Ramsons *Allium ursinum*

Lesser Celandine *Ranunculus ficaria*

Rosebay Willowherb *Epilobium angustifolium*

Thistles *Cirsium sp*

Water Plantain *Alisma plantago-aquatica*

True Bulrush *Scirpus lacustris*

Sweet Chestnut *Castanea sativa*

Acorns *Quercus spp*

by the observant forager from May to July. It is the raw radish-like root that is eaten, and ranges in size from marble to golfball. Fresh and crunchy, it is a favourite spring nibble or salad plant. The plant defends itself from foragers by means of a thread-thin attachment between the stem and tuber, which turns through ninety degrees just as it leaves the tuber. Consequently these tubers can only be harvested by carefully following the stem down to the tuber. The tuber has a thin brown skin which can be easily squeezed off before eating.

Lesser Celandine Ranunculus ficaria: An early spring flower that exploits the light of the forest floor prior to the growth of leaves in the forest canopy. It has small flask shaped tubers up to two centimetres in length which can be harvested in large quantities in the late spring after the flower has begun to die back and the leaves have turned yellow. These must be cooked before eating; boil in two changes of water or roast in hot ashes. No other parts of this plant should be eaten.

Ramsons Allium ursinum: Ramsons are wild onions and frequently announce their presence to the nose before the eye. They can be collected and used like spring onions. However, eaten raw their onion flavour is overpowering: better to collect the tubers and roast them gently in hot embers until golden brown, after which they taste like shallots. Or try braising them in a beef or vegetable stock.

Rosebay Willowherb Epilobium angustifolium: The roots of Rosebay Willowherb can be used for food; however, without careful preparation they will be disappointingly bitter. Collect the roots before the plant flowers, scrape the outside of the root and remove the central brown thread in the root before roasting the roots in hot ashes.

Thistles Cirsium sp: All thistles are edible. Some are perennial, others biennial; whichever, the secret to harvesting succulent roots is to collect them at the completion of their first year's growth. Cook them by roasting in hot ashes.

Water Plantain Alisma plantago-aquatica: Water Plantain's distinctive leaf emerges from mud beside slow flowing water. The root can be gathered and eaten after boiling with two changes of water.

True Bulrush Scirpus lacustris
Club Rush Scirpus maritimus: Both these water plants have edible underground parts which can be eaten after roasting in hot ashes. However, the most productive part of the plant has to be harvested from the deepest water.

Seeds

Next in importance to carbohydrates found in roots and inner bark is that found in the seeds of trees, plants and grasses. Fat hens and melds are heavily endowed with seeds which can be added to stews or soups as a thickening, or dried, then ground with a small amount of water and dribbled on to a hot rock or hot ashes to form a simple bannock. The seeds of Greater Plantain can also be used in this way.

Acorns Quercus spp: One of the most important of all seeds throughout the temperate and semi-arid areas is that from the oak tree. Acorns can be collected by gathering them with leaf litter from underneath the tree. Place this into slow flowing water where the acorns sink and the leaves are carried away. They can then be dried in front of the fire, which will open the shell, and they are then removed laboriously from the shells. The dried and roasted acorn can be used to make coffee, or if you boil the acorn in many changes of water to remove the tannins that turn the water brown they can then be ground up to make a flour substitute, which can be used to make a warming mush cooked with a hot rock or cooked into a bannock in hot ashes.

Sweet Chestnut Castanea sativa*:* Much more palatable than acorns are sweet chestnuts. Can be eaten raw, but at their best cooked. I like to add them to a bannock recipe with crab apple. Delicious.

Hazelnuts Corylus avellana*:* Hazelnuts are usually collected from low bushes. They are at their best when they are just ripe, but you have to beat the squirrels to them, which is not always easy! Delicious raw – you just need to improvise a nutcracker from a fork of a hazel branch.

Walnuts Juglans regia*:* Walnuts, now much less common than they were in the past, are a familiar food and can be collected where there are plenty of walnut trees.

Beechnuts Fagus sylvatica*:* Beechnuts, or beech mast to use the traditional name, are one of my favourite foods. They are very high in oil but the trees do not always produce good kernels. Collect them, then hold them in front of the fire to warm, burst open and reveal the three-sided nut. This has a brown outer layer, which must be broken open to reveal the meat inside.

Grass and Sedge Seeds: Some grasses can be used to produce good seed but you must take care here to ensure there is no black Ergot fungus growing in the seed heads. This infestation is potentially lethal. All sedges are edible. Perhaps the most useful of these is the Pendulous Sedge, which grows in the open shade of temperate woodland. Collect the seed heads, dry, then grind with a small amount of water to a paste, then dribble on to hot ashes or rock and cook as a damper.

GREENS

Nettle Urtica spp*:* The prime green food of the northern temperate zone has to be the stinging nettle. Use only the young leaf tops at the top of the nettle stem. Once cooked they lose the sting. They can be bitter if you don't have any other ingredients to add to them.

Mallow Malva sylvestris*:* Mallow leaves make some of the best soup of all the wild greens, very popular in the Middle East. Today it is usually found growing alongside roads and motorways.

Rosebay Willowherb Epilobium angustifolium*:* The young leaves can be used as a potherb, or dried and used to produce a tea; the young shoots can be steamed then peeled and eaten. The pith can be removed from the mature stalks and used to thicken soups.

Hedge Garlic Alliaria petiolata*:* Hedge Garlic or Jack by the Hedge grows as its name suggests in the dark shade beside hedgerows. It has a very strong garlic flavour and can be used in small quantities in salads or to stuff food steamed under the fire.

Sorrels Oxalis acetosella, Rumex acetosa, Rumex acetosella*:* Wood sorrel, common sorrel and sheep sorrel have an acidic flavour somewhat akin to apple peel and can be used raw in small quantities to improve the flavour of less palatable wild foods or stuffed into fish steamed underground.

Sea Beet Beta vulgaris*:* Sea Beet is often mistaken for spinach, and can be used in exactly the same way. It is found commonly along rivers close to estuaries and along the coastal shoreline.

Sea Purslane Halimione portulacoides*:* Sea Purslane inhabits the salty margins of estuarine rivers, estuaries and mud flats. These fleshy

Walnuts *Juglans regia*

Beechnuts *Fagus sylvatica*

Grass and Sedge Seeds

Nettle *Urtica spp*

Mallow *Malva sylvestris*

Hedge Garlic *Alliaria petiolata*

Oxalis acetosella

Rumex acetosa

Sea Purslane *Halimione portulacoides*

Bilberry *Vaccinium myrtillus*

Elderberry *Sambucus nigra*

Wild Apples *Malus sylvestris*

Rosehips *Rosa canina*

Sloes *Prunus spinosa*

Bullace

Blackberries *Rubus fruticosus*

Raspberry *Rubus idaeus*

salty leaves can be a wonderful addition to a wild meal if lightly steamed first; a particularly good accompaniment to fish caught on the coast such as sea bass.

FRUIT

Bilberries Vaccinium myrtillus: The bilberry grows on low bushes in much of the temperate zone. Bilberries and blueberries are not good for nibbling in a survival situation as they tend to lower the blood sugar, but used with other ingredients, such as bread and bannock mixes with a little sugar, they are wonderful.

Elderberries Sambucus nigra: Elderberries can prove emetic if eaten in large quantities from the bush. Do not confuse the ordinary elderberry with the poisonous dwarf elderberry. Elderberries can be dried and added to bread and bannocks as flavouring, or cooked, or added to stews.

Wild Apples Malus sylvestris: Crab apples are the ancestor of all of our domestic apples, yet because of their bitter taste they are often disregarded. Once cooked they taste like any ordinary apple. They can be collected in large quantities in the autumn. Consider them not just as a survival source of sugar but even a potential addition to some savoury dishes, particularly in risottos with wild mushrooms. Or toast them over the fire until the skin is soft and can be squeezed off.

Rosehips Rosa canina: Rosehips are well known for their vitamin C content. Remember, though that their seeds are covered in tiny hairs, which can irritate the gut, so discard them before eating. Take the bright orange seed cases and infuse them in water for ten or fifteen minutes: drink the rosehip tea, then eat the seed cases. Rosehips can be found throughout the winter.

Sloes Prunus spinosa: Round blue berries the size of a marble that grow on the blackthorn bush. They are very tart and have a high tannin content but this can be greatly reduced by cooking. Deseed and dry them, then add them to bread and bannock mixes.

Bullace: Related to the sloe. Bullace is the tiny wild plum, a delicious wild food, well worth looking out for.

Blackberries Rubus fruticosus: Blackberries need little introduction. They are one of the most common and popular wild foods. Dried blackberry leaves can be used to make a tea.

Raspberry Rubus idaeus: Wild raspberries are to be found in many woodland edges and hedgerows. The leaves mixed with dried blackberry leaves make an acceptable tea.

Cloudberries Rubus chamaemorus: Cloudberries are found mainly in mountainous and moorland regions or in the forests of the very far north. They are a rich-flavoured, orange-looking raspberry growing on a low shrub, more of an Arctic berry, but found sometimes on the edge of the temperate zone.

Cherries Prunus avium, Prunus padus: Wild cherries are very small and the large pit must be removed because it contains cyanide. The flesh is every bit as good as the cultivated variety. The problem is getting to the cherries before the birds do. The wild cherry, Prunus avium, occurs quite high up in the forest canopy and is difficult to reach, but the Bird Cherry, which is more common in the west of the UK, is a shrub, and the cherries can be more easily collected.

FUNGI

Around the world edible fungi are collected in the wild; many are highly prized. In terms of survival education they are frequently ignored, it being suggested that the poor calorific return from fungi does not compensate for the potential risk of collecting a poisonous variety. Some fungi can cause irreversible and fatal poisoning. However, they should not be dismissed: they are rich in minerals, filling and, above all, can transform bland dishes into cordon bleu feasts.

The forager for any wild food must be able to differentiate edible from poisonous. The real problem with fungi is that they can pose more subtle problems in identification than plants. While it is feasible for a novice to teach themselves to identify plants by the sole use of a field guide, it is not wise to attempt this with fungi. If you are interested in eating wild mushrooms you should attend a field study course and learn to identify them accurately. Then a field guide will be infinitely more useful. *Do not eat any fungus unless you are certain of its identification.* For all practical purposes poisonous fungi are *not* rendered safe by cooking. Indeed the testimony of victims reveals that many of the most lethal species actually taste pleasant before and after cooking, including the aptly named Death Cap, *Amanita phalloides*. Lethal fungi are also frequently consumed by animals and invertebrates, but this is not an indication that we can eat them.

IF IN DOUBT – LEAVE IT OUT

Know your poisonous fungi

The most poisonous fungi belong to the Death Cap family *Amanitaceae*, of which there are over twenty species to be found within the UK. Not all members of the family are poisonous: Caesar's Mushroom, *Amanita caesarea* (not found in the UK) is one of the most sought after edible mushrooms. However, for survival purposes we err on the side of caution, considering all members of this family to be poisonous. Members of this family possess characteristic features that you should learn to recognise. (see page 199).

Poisonous Amanitas

- The Death Cap *Amanita phalloides*
- Destroying Angel *Amanita virosa*
- Fly Agaric *Amanita muscaria*
- Panther Cap *Amanita pantherina*
- The Blusher *Amanita rubescens*
- Grisette *Amanita vaginata*
- Tawny Grisette *Amanita fulva*
- The Spring Amanita *Amanita verna*
- *Amanita echinocephala*
- *Amanita gemmata*

Other poisonous families

Apart from the Death Cap family there are many other poisonous fungi to be avoided. Certain other families pose a threat to the unwary forager, most notably the:

- Cortinarius family *Cortiariaceae* (particularly *Cortinarius speciosissimus* and *Cortinarius orellanus*)

Also included in the family are:

- The Inocybe family (particularly the Red Staining Inocybe *Inocybe patouillardii*)
- The Hebeloma family

In addition to these families the following species have been mistaken for edible species:

- False Morel *Gyromitra esculenta*
- *Entoloma sinuatum*
- Yellow Stainer *Agaricus xanthoderma*
- Brown Roll-rim *Paxillus involutus*
- Satan's Boletus *Boletus satanus*
- *Boletus erythropus*
- *Boletus luridus*
- Woolly Milk Cap *Lactarius torminosus*
- *Lactarius pubescens*
- Common Earthball *Scleroderma citrinum*

Death Cap (Amanita phalloides): note the basal sac reaching up the stem, the white skirt beneath the cap and the olive green colour of the cap.

1. A universal veil which encloses the immature fruit body.

   In some species (such as the Fly Agaric *Amanita muscaria* and Panther Cap *Amanita pantherina*) remnants of this remain as white spots/scales on the cap surface of the mature fungus. These spots/scales can be easily brushed off or washed away by rain.

2. A skirt or ring under the cap.

   In other species (such as the Death Cap *Amanita phalloides*, and Grisette *Amanita vaginata*) remnants of the universal veil remain as a basal sac or volva.

   A skirt is commonly found around the stem beneath the cap, although it is sometimes absent

3. All members of this family have white spores.

   These can sometimes be seen in the characteristic gill pattern coating leaves beneath the toadstool. If not they can be observed by placing the cap on to a smooth dark surface overnight. The spores of poisonous *Amanitas* are also extremely poisonous.

4. All British species have white/cream gills, free of the stem.

5. Cap colour varies
   • Olive-green cap for the Death Cap *Amanita phalloides*.
   • White for Destroying Angel *Amanita virosa*.
   • Red for Fly Agaric *Amanita muscaria*.
   • Brown for Panther Cap *Amanita pantherina*.

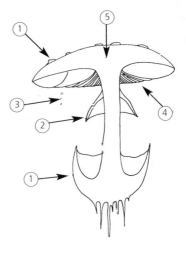

- *Scleroderma verrucosum*
- Sulphur Tuft *Hypholoma fasiculare*
- False Chanterelle *Hygrophoropsis aurantiaca*
- The Sickener *Russula emetica*
- Beechwood Sickener *Russula mairei*

Most cases of poisoning occur when toxic species are confused with edible species, and a useful question to ask of the victims or their mushroom-picking benefactors is the identity of the mushroom they thought they were picking. In the absence of a well-preserved specimen, the answer to this question could narrow the possible suspects considerably.

SENSITIVITY: some people are undoubtedly sensitive to some kinds of mushrooms, especially if eaten raw, e.g. the Wood Blewit *Lepista nuda*, and Chicken of the Woods *Laetiporus sulpureus*.

Collecting fungi for food

Many fungi are good eating, and if care and caution is exercised a large proportion of them can be identified in the field by eye.

When you are collecting fungi for eating follow these rules to avoid making unnecessary mistakes in identification:

1. Do not collect baby/button stage fungi. It can be difficult to positively identify immature fungi.
2. Handle the fungus carefully to prevent damage that may impair its identification.
3. Make certain that you have all of the fungus; the base of the stem can be vital to correct identification.
4. Do not collect old or decaying fungi. Fungi that are old can be difficult to identify correctly because their colours change and their distinguishing features become damaged.
5. Do not eat any fungus unless you are 100% certain of its identification.
6. When collecting do not mix poisonous with edible species.

7. Having positively identified an edible fungus always cook it before eating.

IF IN DOUBT – LEAVE IT OUT

Fungi growing from the ground

With a spongy layer under the cap

These fungi are generally referred to as 'Boletus' fungi. They are very prized and collected in many countries in large numbers. They are one of the safest forms of fungi for beginners. If you cut the cap in half you will see that the sponge-like layer is comprised of many parallel tubes. Some of these fungi will exhibit a rapid colour change to blue on cutting or bruising; this is not an indicator of the edibility of the fungus.

- Penny Bun *Boletus edulis*
- Bitter Bolete *Tylopilus felleus*
- Bay Boletus *Xerocomus badius*
- Summer Boletus *Boletus aereus*
- Brown Birch Boletus *Leccinum scabrum*
- Orange Birch Boletus *Leccinum versipelle*
- Oak Boletus *Leccinum quercinum*
- Aspen Boletus *Leccinum aurantiacum*
- Slippery Jack *Suillus luteus*
- Larch Bolete *Suillus bovinus*

With spines under the cap

These fungi are generally referred to as 'Hedgehog' fungi. Within the UK none is poisonous although some are too tough to eat.

Hedgehog Fungus Hydnum repandum:
Yellowish with pale flesh coloured cap. Can grow in large numbers. Deciduous and coniferous woodland. Excellent eating.

Hedgehog Fungus Hydnum rufescens:
Salmony orange-brown cap. Can grow in large numbers. Deciduous and coniferous woodland. Excellent eating.

Brown Birch Boletus
Leccinum scabrum

Penny Bun *Boletus edulis*

Penny Bun (alternative form).

Bitter Bolete
Tylopilus felleus

Bay Boletus
Xerocomus badiu

Oak Boletus
Leccinum quercinum

Slippery Jack
Suillus luteus

Hedgehog Fungus *Hydnum repandum*

Horn of Plenty
Craterellus cornucopides

Giant Puffball
Langermannia gigantea

Calvatia utriformis

The Common Puffball
Lycoperdon perlatum

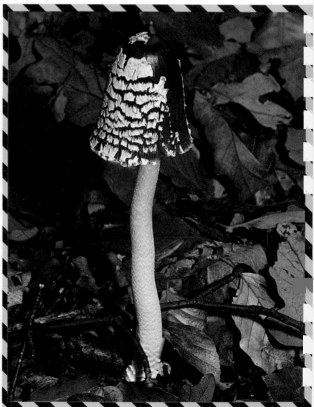

Judge's Wig/Shaggy Inkcap
Coprinus comatus

Magpie Inkcap – not edible.
Coprinus picaceus

Sarcodon imbricatum: Velvety reddish-purplish brown cap, cracking into overlapping scales (not removable). Pale flesh coloured background. Most frequent in Scottish pine forests.

Trumpet shaped without gills, sponge or spines

Horn of Plenty Craterellus cornucopides: Black trumpet-like fungus fading grey with age. Often found in large groups in leaf litter. They dry well and are good flavouring for a survival stew.

Ball shaped fungi

Ball shaped fungi are called puffballs because of the way they disperse their spores. Before they mature to this puffing stage they can be collected for food.

Puffball guidelines

The flesh of a puffball must be pure white when cut through without any signs of the development of other features.

AVOID:

- Puffballs that have a yellow or purple colour inside or that have turned to spores.

- Earthballs which can be mistaken for puffballs. These have a rubbery outer layer and a rich cream interior when very young which turns deep purple to black inside as the fungus matures.

- Button stage fungi that show the shape of the developing toadstool.

Giant Puff Ball Langermannia gigantea: The Giant puffball is difficult to mistake, a large round white fungus most often about the size of a football. When cut through it should exhibit smooth, firm, textured, creamy white flesh with no signs of any features such as stem or gills developing internally.

Calvatia utriformis: A white ball-shaped fungus about the size of a tennis ball with a short stubby stem.

The Common Puffball Lycoperdon perlatum: A white puffball about the size of a ping-pong ball, with a short stem. Its outer surface is covered with tiny spines that brush off easily.

The Stump Puffball Lycoperdon pyriforme: A beige to brown coloured puffball slightly smaller than a ping-pong ball with a short stem. This puffball only grows on wood which may be buried in leaf litter.

Fungi with gills
(like the common/true mushroom0

Most poisonings occur with gill bearing fungi. Particularly when confused for the true mushroom or the chanterelle.

IF IN DOUBT –
LEAVE THE GILLED FUNGI OUT

True Mushrooms: The true mushroom MUST have a ring round the stem and MUST have gills turning pink to chocolate.

One member of the mushroom family can give alarming symptoms of sweating and stomach cramps —Yellow Stainer *Agaricus xanthoderma.* This is a true mushroom but when handled or bruised it turns a very bright yellow and has an unpleasant smell of carbolic. It does not affect everyone, but it is best avoided. It is frequently found on the margin of deciduous woodland.

Judge's Wig/Shaggy Ink Cap Coprinus comatus: A very distinctive fungus like its common name. Also known as Shaggy Ink Cap because of the large white scales with brownish tips. This fungus is upright and all white in colour. (Do not confuse it with the black and white capped Magpie Ink Cap Coprinus picaceus.) Eat only young specimens, before the gills have started to dissolve into the inky spore-bearing liquid.

Parasol Mushroom **Lepiota procera:** A very large fungus with an excellent taste. Sometimes almost as big as a dinner plate. Cream coloured gills and cap with shaggy scales (scales cannot be brushed off). The stem has a large double 'sliding' ring and snake-like markings.

Shaggy Parasol **Lepiota rhacodes:** A similar fungus to *L.procera*, cream coloured gills, cap with very shaggy scales (scales cannot be brushed off). The stem has a large double 'sliding' ring but without the snake-like markings. Flesh turns red on cutting. Although

also edible it can cause stomach upsets in some people.

Chanterelle **Cantharellus cibarius:** A wonderful fungus to find which is seldom wormy and one of the best edible species. It can grow in large numbers in woodland, often near pine. It is a wavy edged trumpet-shaped fungus with egg-yellow gills, which more resemble veins running down the stem. Smells of apricots. The stem is robust and tends to snap cleanly when bent.

Honey Fungus **Armillaria mellea:** This fungus can be found in large areas of woodland and can grow in dense clusters at the base of trees. Although edible, honey fungus can be mildly toxic if eaten raw, so it must be cooked, even if only boiled up for a few minutes (the water then discarded). Honey fungus is very varied in form but generally speaking, as the name suggests, is honey-coloured and has gills off-white to dark

RISKS OF CONFUSION

Chanterelle is one of the most sought after of edible fungi; inevitably there have been deaths and serious poisonings when the unwary have mistaken it for other species. Particularly *Cortinarius speciosissimus*, *Cortinarius orellanus*, neither of which has gills running down the stem and have a distinctive radishy scent.

More easily mistaken for Chanterelle is the False Chanterelle, *Hygrophoropsis aurantiaca*, which can grow near to the true chanterelle. This has a more red-orange colour, more blade like gills which do run down the stem. The stem is more flexible and tends to green-stick fracture when bent. The scent of apricots is absent.

In the USA Chanterelle can be confused with Jack O'Lantern *Omphalotus illudens*. This has crowded bright orange blade-like gills that run down the stem, but lacks the distinctive apricot odour of Chanterelle. An unusual feature of this fungus is that fresh the gills glow a bright greenish yellow in the dark.

Parasol Mushroom
Lepiota procera

Shaggy Parasol
Lepiota rhacodes

Chanterelle
Cantharelus cibarius

Honey Fungus
Armillaria mellea

The Cauliflower Fungus
Sparassis crispa

Chicken of the Woods
Laetiporus sulphureus

brown. The stem has a ring. Several other fungus species grow in groups in this manner and can be harmful (in particular the toxic Sulphur Tuft *Hypholoma fasiculare*, which has sulphur-coloured gills) so care must be taken in the identification of this species. IF IN DOUBT LEAVE HONEY FUNGUS OUT.

Fungi growing on trees
At the base of mature Scots Pine Trees

The Cauliflower Fungus Sparassis crispa:
20–50cm across. Found usually in a large clump at the base of mature Scots pines or

nearby. This soft, rubbery, brain-like fungus is very distinctive and large specimens will last for days. Portions dry well hung up on strings. Excellent eating.

On the trunks of standing mature trees above waist height

Chicken of the Woods Laetiporus sulphureus:
15–50cm across. A spectacular fungus growing mostly on yew, cherry, sweet chestnut, oak and mature willow. Brilliant yellow to orange with a velvet-like texture, it usually grows in tiers and resembles polystyrene pouring out

Ox Tongue or Beef Steak
Fungus *Fistulina hepatica*

Oyster Fungus
Pleurotus ostreatus

Pleurotus cornucopiae

of the tree. It darkens with age before eventually fading white when it dries. Best sliced finely and fried or added to a survival stew.

Ox Tongue or Beef Steak Fungus Fistulina hepatica*: As its name suggests it resembles a large liver or tongue. It usually grows above shoulder height on oak and sweet chestnut trees, large logs and stumps. When cut through it looks like steak and has a blood-like sap. Bitter to taste, it is best sliced into chunks soaked in salt water for at least two hours before kebabing with other wild foods. Eaten hot it resembles steak.

Oyster Fungus Pleurotus ostreatus*: 6–14cm across. Blue-grey shell shaped fungus growing in clusters, one on top of the other. Found on the trunks and stumps of dead or decaying trees, particularly beech, often in large masses.

Pleurotus cornucopiae: Similar to *P. ostreatus* but with a cream colour and growing usually on oak, beech and elm.

Growing on the stems and branches of elder

Jew's Ear Auricularia auricula judae*: 2–4 cm across. This brown ear-like fungus is easily recognised, particularly when growing on elder. Rubbery and elastic, its outer surface is velvety. In dry weather it shrinks and dries hard, in which state it can be picked and stored for rehydrating by soaking in warm water or dropping into the survival stew at a later time.

Jew's Ear *Auricularia auricula judae*

LICHEN

This is perhaps one of the most unlikely food resources. In biological terms lichen are distinct organisms, based on a symbiotic relationship between fungi and algae. Some lichen are edible and have been used as food in times of famine, while others are eaten as a rare delicacy. They can sometimes be found in great quantity, but you will use a lot of energy in cleaning them. Only a few species of lichen are toxic, such as wolf lichen, *Letharia vulpina*.

Slow-growing edible lichen should be collected for food only in times of extreme shortage and where they grow in abundance. They contain acids which make them unpalatable and, more seriously, can cause an emetic reaction. The acids can be neutralised by boiling them in a solution of bicarbonate of soda or, if this is not available, an alkaline solution made by boiling wood ash in water. Strain the lichen, then boil again in fresh water. They are an unappealing foodstuff with little flavour, but can be added to other wild foods for their carbohydrate.

Iceland Moss Cetraria islandica*: This lichen is common in Arctic and sub-Arctic regions. Boil it in several changes of water then dry it to reduce the bitterness. Powder it and boil it again. Skim off any scum before consumption. Flavour is decidedly lacking, so use the lichen broth as the base of a soup made with other more flavourful ingredients.

Old Man's Beard Lichen Alectoria sp *and* Bryoria sp*: Like cotton wool, these lichen festoon trees in the far north. They are commonly used as tinder but can also be eaten. Collect the lichen and pick out as many needles and twigs as possible, then boil in a solution of bicarbonate of soda or wood ash. In British Columbia these lichen were cooked in ground ovens in layers with wild onion bulbs.

Lichen has to be one of the most unlikely sources of food.

Rock Tripe Umbillicaria*: The most unlikely-looking edible lichen. Dark greeny grey, it covers rocky surfaces in the north. Leathery when moist, it is brittle when dry and the most acidic of the edible lichens. After collecting the lichen wash out the grit and dry it, then boil in a solution of bicarbonate of soda or wood ash.

Reindeer Moss Cladonia sp*: This lichen thrives in sandy conditions, particularly on the tundra. Grey-green in colour it is multi-branched, growing in tufts, which can be extensive. As its name suggests, it is the food of reindeer, which dig down and graze it from under snow in the winter. Wash and boil or fry it.

SEAWEED

The majority of us have direct contact with seaweed only when walking on the shoreline, or delving into rock pools. Usually it appears lifeless and rubbery in unappealing colours. When it rots, seaweed attracts clouds of flies and gives off a repellent odour. To appreciate seaweed, we must get into the water with it. The best time to do this is in the warm summer months, when seaweed growth is at its height. Arrange to be on a beach at low water of a spring tide: spring tides occur fortnightly throughout the year in the UK but are most extreme in March and September. At these times more of the seabed is exposed than at other times in the year.

Seaweed species prefer different zones of the shore: some, such as *Chorda filum*, thrive in areas of permanent water while others, like *Enteromorpha intestinalis*, tolerate exposure at low tide and therefore proliferate on the upper part of a beach. Choose an area that will not be cut off by the rising tide and snorkel with the seaweeds as the tide rises.

It has been stated that all species of seaweed are edible, but this is not strictly true: while the majority are edible some are not worth eating and a few, notably the *Desmarestia aculeata* and *Desmarestia lingulata* species (sometimes referred to as sea sorrels), are too acidic. However, the best and most common edible seaweeds are very easily recognised.

Seaweeds are rich in minerals, particularly iodine, and also contain notable amounts of protein and carbohydrate. In most cases 10 per cent or more, of the dried weight of seaweed is comprised of protein and over 50 per cent carbohydrate. However, only a small proportion of the carbohydrate is digestible – in fact unless one is accustomed to eating seaweeds it is wise at first to only eat small amounts as they have a well-established reputation as a purgative. They are also quite filling.

The vitamin content of seaweeds is quite astonishing: 100g of an average seaweed can provide over half your daily requirement of vitamin C, and more than the daily requirement of vitamins A, B2, B12, sodium, potassium and magnesium. They also contains chlorine, calcium and vitamin D.

Sea Lettuce Ulva lactuca: Without a doubt, Sea Lettuce is the most appetising seaweed to look at: its bright emerald green is somewhat reminiscent of lettuce leaves. Its other common name is green laver. I like to eat it raw, cut up into small segments and included in seafood salads. Dried and chopped up finely it is a pleasing addition to seafood soup.

Dulse Palmaria palmata: Dulse has beautiful translucent red fronds, a treat added raw to a wild salad. It is crispy-textured with a wonderful ocean flavour. Dried, it can be ground to a powder and used as a salt substitute. It has a high protein content and contains all of the trace elements we need. Rolled into tight tubes and dried, dulse make an excellent savoury trail snack for hikers.

Sweet Oarweed
Laminaria saccharina

Laver
Porphyra umbilicaris

Egg Wrack
Ascophyllum nodosum

Surprisingly it is excellent deep-fried like potato crisps.

Irish Moss/Carrageen Chondrus crispus; Gigartina stellata: Irish moss releases gelatine when boiled, as does the similar seaweed *Gigartina stellata.* They can be used to produce nourishing if bland tasting jelly or to thicken soup or make blancmange: wash a good handful of the seaweed in clean water, tie it into a piece of cheesecloth with a vanilla pod and cook it for 30 minutes with 1 litre of milk in a bain-marie. Remove the cheesecloth, sweeten, and chill.

Enteromorpha intestinalis: A delicate emerald green seaweed that floats in the high-water region of a beach; it can be easily found and used as Sea Lettuce.

Sweet Oarweed Laminaria saccharina*:*
Common, and good eating, particularly the fresh young stipes cooked in a little water or steamed. As its name suggests it contains a

sugar, mannitol, which crystallises when the seaweed dries.

Laver Porphyra umbilicaris*:* Laver resembles a piece of old polythene more than an edible food, but it is widely considered excellent eating. It is the best known of our edible seaweeds. Laver bread takes time and effort to produce and I prefer to dry laver and eat it like dulse or diced in soups as for sea lettuce.

Egg Wrack Ascophyllum nodosum*:* The Egg or Knotted Wrack is an unlikely looking food: tough rubbery fronds with large egg-shaped flotation chambers. With a high fat and oil content, it has a delicate flavour after cooking in a little water or steaming. Only use the tenderest young samples.

Gathering Seaweed
Don't just empty the shore: cut young healthy specimens leaving the holdfast attached to the rock with plenty of frond.

SHELLFISH

Shellfish provide rich and easily collected food and can be found in fresh- and salt-water environments.

Shrimps

Marine shrimps are traditionally collected by either scooping them from the sea at low tide using hand nets, or further out to sea using trammel nets. On remote shorelines it is possible to improvise a shrimping net from a mosquito net attached to an H-shaped frame of light wood which can be towed through the surf.

Freshwater shrimps are mostly found in a useful size in warm tropical waters: most shallow streams in rainforests contain them. They can be collected with a mosquito headnet converted into a dip net or stretched taut in a frame. Disturb the leaf litter in the stream to flush out the shrimps, then scoop them up with your net a little way downstream.

Crabs, lobsters, squat lobsters and crayfish

Crabs, lobsters and crayfish provide some of the tastiest wild food. However, without access to a boat and crab or lobster pots, it is unlikely that you will find large crabs or lobsters, although in tropical regions large mud crabs can be speared in rock pools at low tide. Even so it is well worth searching rock pools for smaller crabs, and at very low tide turning over rocks in search of squat lobsters. A hooked stick or crooked piece of metal rod can be a great help in hooking them out of their retreats. You can improvise a trap for crab and lobster from strong fishing line and saplings. Make a hoop of flexible sapling or vines and reinforce it with two spokes crossing at its centre. Knot nooses made from fishing line around the circumference, then attach a weight and bait – dead rotting oily fish is ideal – at the centre. Lower this from rocks at high tide or anchor it to the seabed at low tide and

recover it at the next low tide. In trying to reach the bait, the crabs and lobsters become entangled in the snares. In clear water it may be possible to collect crabs by improvising a drop net, baited in the same way. Attach a mosquito net or a piece of old fishing net to a weighted frame. Lower it on to the seabed, watch it, and when crabs scramble over it, lift it. In England the same method has been used in less clear water using an old bicycle wheel as the frame for the drop net. Bait and lower it into a likely spot for 10–20 minutes then haul it up swiftly to the surface. In the tropics crabs are frequently to be found in freshwater streams. The classic method for catching crayfish is to take an old bucket or large tin can and punch pencil-diameter holes into the sides and bottom so that it will sink, or use a chicken-wire mesh drum. Bait it with old meat, the smellier the better, and submerge it close to a river bank. Crayfish are skilled trap robbers: to foil them remove the trap before daylight.

Bivalves

Bivalve shellfish include some of the most popular *fruits de mer*, like mussels, oysters and clams. However, you must exercise caution in eating them. Bivalvular shellfish are filter feeders: they strain nutrients from water passed through a siphon organ, and may contain pollutants, especially mussels, which live in open water, so filter more than clams, which live in nutrient-rich silt and sand. For the most part pathogenic bacteria are destroyed in cooking as long as the shellfish are cooked at 100 degrees Celsius for longer than 20 minutes, or for a shorter time in the much hotter embers of an open fire.

The toxin most responsible for shellfish poisoning is a marine algae of the *Gonyaulax* genus. When prevalent in large numbers, the algae become visible, turning the coastal water a reddish brown. Hence the term applied to their presence, 'red tides'. Unfortunately, they

Top: Many shellfish can be cooked simply in the embers of your campfire.

Bottom left: Wild crayfish caught with a headnet in a small stream.

Bottom right: Large jungle crayfish. One of the joys of remote wilderness can be an abundance of wild food, a lesson in conservation.

Top left: Spend enough time in the company of hunter-gatherers and you become alert to a wealth of potential food sources, such as these freshwater mussels.

Top right: These clams, called 'white mussels' in Namibia, are arranged for cooking. Hot ashes and embers are laid over them; as they cook the meat shrinks back towards the hinge and away from the sand.

Bottom left: In the urban world we are far removed from the reality of the life of hunter-gatherers. Consider the demands of raising children. In the billy can is a meal of freshwater crabs collected in the headwaters of the Orinoco River.

Bottom right: Limpets are an undervalued source of food.

can be present in sufficient quantity to pose a serious threat to our health yet not be visible to the naked eye. Red tides cause two forms of poisoning: diarrhoetic shellfish poisoning (DSP), which causes serious illness , and paralytic shellfish poisoning (PSP), which is life-threatening and leads to paralysis and the ultimate failure of our vital organs. Local knowledge of seasons when these tides occur is the only way to predict them. Hikers foraging along shorelines should stay alert to fishery authorities' advice and warnings. Bivalve shellfish also concentrate chemical pollutants after shipwrecks.

Mussels

Marine mussels are easily collected from rocks at low tide. They should be cleaned up and kept overnight in fresh water. The next day check that they are still healthy before you cook them. Squeeze the shell slightly open: healthy mussels will close again, tight shut. Discard any mussels that remain closed after cooking by steaming or boiling for at least 20 minutes, or for less time in the embers of an open fire. Discard any that do not open up during cooking.

Freshwater mussels

Found in rivers with silty beds – look for old shells washed up on sandbars along the river. You will frequently encounter them when searching for aquatic food plants, such as the tubers of arrowhead *Sagittaria*.

Clams

Clams and cockles can be raked or dug from sand or silt at low tide depending upon the species. They can be treated in the same way as mussels.

Razor-shells are only available at the lowest tides and they can dig themselves rapidly into the sand to evade you; you must employ special means to capture them. My favourite method is to approach their distinctive keyhole-shaped opening in the sand stealthily and sprinkle salt, or squirt a concentrated salt-water solution, into the hole. After a few seconds the razor-shell will project upwards through the hole by a couple of centimetres. Grasp it with your thumb and index finger, but do not pull. You will feel the razor-shell attempt to escape but soon it will exhaust itself and relax. Then you can draw it out easily.

Univalve shellfish

Includes whelks, limpets and winkles. Whelks are usually trapped in baited basket traps and, with the exception of the occasional whelk trapped in rock pools at extreme low tide, are usually beyond the reach of foragers. They may be affected by the red-tide organism (see page 210) as they eat filter feeders.

Limpets are one of the most reliable survival foods. As grazers, they are less prone to pollutants than filter feeders. They are not collected commercially because they are difficult to harvest and their texture is rough and chewy. However, neither is reason enough for a forager to discard them. To collect limpets, strike them swiftly and firmly with a rock to dislodge them. Use stealth and surprise: if you are unsuccessful on your first attempt they will clamp down extra hard.

To cook them, either place them upside down in a shallow bed of embers or allow them to clamp down on to a flat rock or metal sheet over which you ignite a rapid hot fire of dry grass or small twigs. When they are cooked the shell will easily lift free. Cut away the black blister, which contains the internal organs, and eat the orange mussel-like meat. They can be made into kebabs or even diced and used in a chowder.

Winkles are still a treat in coastal Britain. Boil them for 20–30 minutes and then use a pin to lift off their watertight seal and extract the spirally body. The same process is used elsewhere with mangrove snails and telescopium snails.

Sea urchins

Sea urchins are frequently a thorn in the forager's foot, but a popular seafood, particularly in the Mediterranean. They are boiled or steamed then broken open to reveal the soft edible interior.

Octopus

Octopus are usually harvested by spear fishermen, although occasionally they can be found in rock pools. Turn them inside out to kill them. To cook, boil or stew them in marinades made from fruit or coconut cream.

INSECTS

Today the idea of eating an insect is repulsive to many people, yet historically insects have been an important source of human nutrition. Indeed, in many tropical countries indigenous peoples still relish insect foods. High in nutritional content, insects are an easily digested source of protein.

Caterpillars

Generally, caterpillars are toxic, which is recognisable from their bright colour or irritant hairs. Never handle hairy caterpillars: they can cause serious, long-lasting skin rashes. In Africa the mopane caterpillar, the larval stage of the mopane moth, *Gonimbrasia belina*, is spiny, hairless, yellow, red and black, 6–8cm long and found in large numbers on the mopane tree. They can be eaten raw, sun-dried or cooked. Discard the head before eating.

Witchetty grubs

Several different species of witchetty grub are eaten by Aboriginal people in Australia. They are found in the roots of the witchetty bush – you will know they're there if you can find the empty cases of emergent moths below it. Excavate the roots of the bush and look for 15mm diameter holes in them. Break open the roots and collect the grubs. They can be eaten

raw or cooked quickly in hot ashes. They taste of scrambled eggs.

Palm grubs

Large white palm grubs are found in the trunks of fallen sago and other palms. They are such an important food source that some peoples deliberately fell palm trees to create a habitat for them. When you cut into the soft palm wood, look for 2–3cm diameter holes, which betray their presence. They can be eaten raw or cooked and have a pleasant palm oil flavour.

Teredo worms

The Teredo, mangrove or ship worm inhabits dead timber in the marine environment, particularly mangrove wood. They are easily found by chopping into dead mangrove wood beside any 8–10cm diameter holes. A mollusc, this borer is one of the least appealing of all edible grubs but tastes good. Eaten raw it is rather like crab.

Ants

Ants are eaten in many parts of the world, particularly the green ant in Australia, which tastes of lemon and has antibiotic properties. During summer in the northern temperate

Top and bottom left: Teredo worms were a bane to ancient mariners, boring through ships' timbers, despite their appearance they taste fine . . . really.

Top right: Witchetty grubs — delicious.

Bottom right: Palm grubs are even tastier than witchetty grubs.

Opposite page: 'Wood ants' nests are a lesson in shelter building.

1. Cast nest and larvae on to tarp – do not use all of the nest.

2. Fold over the tarp edge to create shade.

3. The ants do the work for you – after 20–30 minutes open up the shade and hey presto.

zone wood ant larvae will make an emergency meal. Fried gently they taste of shrimp. To collect them trick the ants into doing the work. Lay your tarp next to the ants' nest and break open the nest, casting the larvae, nest material and ants on to the centre of the tarp. Lay some sticks around the edge of the tarp and fold over the sides to create shade. The ants will collect up the larvae and deposit them in the shade. After 20 minutes fold back the tarp edges and scoop up the larvae, which look like puffed rice.

Honey ants taste like barley sugar.

Earthworms
In dire emergency the humble earthworm has been used as a source of protein. British POWs used them to supplement their meagre rations while forced to labour on the Burma railroad. They kept the worms in salt water, massaging them until they had purged and were pink in colour. They can also be sun-dried and powdered for use in bouillon.

Slugs and snails
Slugs are generally best avoided as they feed on poisonous fungi and may also become toxic.

Snails are widely eaten. In the tropics giant land snails are sold in the markets in bundles of five with a liana tie passed through holes in the shells. In Europe, the giant Roman snail, commonly found on chalky downs, and the smaller common grey snail are edible. It is best to purge them by keeping them for several days and feeding them only dandelion or wild garlic leaves. If you are confident that they have not been feeding on toxic plants, you can cook them immediately. Cooked Aboriginal style in hot embers until their juices boil over they are a tasty if chewy delicacy.

Amphibians and reptiles
A wide range of amphibians are eaten, from crocodiles to frogs. In an emergency, frogs are easy to catch but only the hind legs are worth eating. All members of the *Rana* genus are edible. Beware of tropical frogs, which may be highly toxic, such as arrow-poison frogs. Toads are toxic, although they were used as food in Britain's rural past. Remove the dangerous paratoid glands, situated behind the eyes, and gut them before cooking. Today, with ever-

Happy with this meal, the San bushman heads home to share this lizard with his family.

disappearing wetland habitats, many amphibians are protected by law – and I would far rather watch them than eat them!

Lizards and snakes are eaten in many parts of the world, caught either by snare or spear. They are white-fleshed and good eating.

BIRDS

One of the most delightful aspects of outdoors life is the constant presence of our feathered cousins, but of course in an emergency they may also be an important food source. The best-known food species are ducks, geese, grouse, pheasants and pigeons, although many smaller birds are eaten by indigenous peoples. Eggs can also be collected, most easily found in wetland habitats. Birds are protected by law from poaching, but in a true emergency these traps from our pre-industrial past may save the day.

When using birds as food, do not drink their blood or eat raw flesh: they are prone to parasitic infestation.

Old English bird trap.

FISHING

Many a skilled fisherman has used rod and line to feed a party in the wilds after the food stocks have been damaged or lost. Conventional fishing techniques are a useful and important aspect of wilderness travel. In my experience lure and worm fishing are the most widely successful techniques: a good reel, a good-quality line, a carriage rod (in several sections) and a selection of hooks and lures need not be heavy and bulky. Make sure that you have the required licence and that you follow the authorities' guidelines on species and size. The rules are intended to safeguard the river ecology, which is, after all, what we are there to enjoy.

Here are some techniques commonly employed in the wilderness when fishing for food and not sport. On civilised waters they may be considered bad practice or prohibited. However, in remote areas where pressure on fish stocks is virtually non-existent they remain an appropriate means of fishing for food.

Where to look for fish

Before considering the fishing method, you must look for the most productive water in your vicinity. Finding fish is essentially a commonsense process: if it is hot and sunny look for cool shady pools; if it is cold, seek warm, sunny spots. Check deep eddies on fast-moving streams, particularly where insects falling from overhanging vegetation may offer a popular feeding place. When water babbles or gushes over rocks it becomes oxygenated: the oxygen-rich water below can provide first-rate fishing opportunities, as can nutrient-rich areas of rivers, such as where a stream joins a river. On wide open water look for narrows – for example, between islands or between an island and the shore where the fish will be funnelled into a smaller area. Observe the behaviour and movements of other wildlife: herons, pelicans, otters and many other expert

Top left: In Lapland a Sami man sets a snare for Ptarmigan.

Top right: Detail of the bushman Koran trap – note tree gum used as bait.

Bottom right: In Namibia a San bushman sets a snare for a Koran bird.

fisher creatures may point the way to your own success.

Indicators of fish feeding
The most obvious sign is fish breaking the surface to take insects. However, many species stay close to the bottom, grazing on vegetation and molluscs, disturbing vegetation, which rises to the water surface.

When to fish
Generally, early morning, late afternoon, twilight and at night are the most productive times, but here experimentation will be your best guide.

Left: Wild brown trout are a delicious meal, a gift of nature to the respectful fisherman.

Tickling

Tickling, or guddling as it is known in Scotland, is a widely prohibited method of fishing. In the past, tickling was the high art of non-commercial poaching, and no other method of fishing is so primal or as satisfying. Tickling was employed in two types of water: the first in shallow water to take fish almost beached on their way to spawn, the easiest method, and still used on the Falkland Islands; the second in rivers with clear water, shady pools and overhanging banks. Classically the fish is gently encouraged into a shady pool where it takes refuge under a bank. Then wading slowly and gently, with your hands submerged in front of you, palms up, reach under the bank exploring with your fingertips. Amazingly, you will eventually discover the gentle flick of a fin and the belly of the fish. The first time you do this you will certainly flinch and scare the fish away. The second time, however, you will be ready. Having found the fish, the secret is to move your palms under its belly, then swiftly and without hesitation snatch it with a enfolding grip that bends it preventing its escape. Draw the fish towards your stomach and cast it well up on to the bank. Many a fish has escaped by wriggling back into the water.

Strangely enough trout taste best poached.

Bailing

A technique I have seen employed in tropical Africa. A section of small slow-flowing stream is dammed off in two places and the water between the dams bailed out to reveal the bed.

As the water level drops, the fish take refuge under stones, logs and any crevice they can find. They must be winkled out from in hidey-holes, which is surprisingly difficult. It must be the least skilful fishing technique, but effective none the less.

Driving – lau

In Western Samoa I had the opportunity to take part in a lau. This involves a group effort. Before low tide people gather on the beach and make a long rope of vines and coconut-palm leaves to use as a corral: the palm leaves are spliced in so that they will hang down in the water like a screen. When it is ready the lau is taken out into the water at low tide, held by people 4 – 5 metres apart. The party gradually creates a circle at least 100 metres in diameter. The reef fish are trapped inside the corral as they are not prepared to pass the leaf screen. When the circle is complete, spear fishermen enter it and catch the trapped fish. Afterwards the catch is divided between the participants, and with the wisdom of generations, the reef just fished is left until the stocks have recovered.

Spearing

Today spearing survives only in remote communities where fishing is solely a matter of food collecting. Of the many methods I have encountered the technique that most impresses me is that of the Aboriginal peoples of northern Australia, who use a long, light spear with four splayed metal tines 40cm long. Traditionally made from hardwood bound with banyan fibre and beeswax, metal and copper wire or strong mono-filament fishing lines are now the norm. This easily made hunting tool is used to catch fish, rays, crabs, longnecked turtles, lizards, birds, crayfish. It is enhanced by the use of a *woomera* (spear-thrower), which increases the speed of throwing, aids accuracy and, if necessary, can impart greater force to the spear. To use this

weapon requires considerably more skill than a modern hunting tool. For example, when hunting rays you learn quickly that tidal conditions must be in your favour, just on the ebb so that the water is clear with good visibility and not sandy. Then you have to move slowly with stealth and recognise the subtlest disturbance in the pattern of the seabed that betrays the presence of the ray. Once they are seen, you must throw with accuracy and without hesitation. The *woomera* serves as the club to dispatch the prey. When hunting among Aboriginal people, you will not easily detect any obvious process of conservation, but each hunter's hand is guided by ancient wisdom, a process of conservation enshrined in strictly observed Aboriginal law that dictates which species each hunter may or may not hunt.

In the tropics, on reefs and in forest streams, simple harpoons are put to great use. To succeed with them you need swimming goggles or a diving mask. Today harpoons are usually powered by rubber, either with a spear and catapult-like arrangement or, more commonly, with a loop of rubber attached to the tail of a spear with several tines. To fire it the thumb is passed through the loop of rubber, which is stretched, and the spear grasped well up its shaft. Releasing the shaft causes the harpoon to shoot forward. A simple and effective fishing method.

Angling

Angling or fishing with a hook and line is the most widespread fishing method, and if you are travelling on water you should consider taking a rod and lures with you, or improvising a simple rod from a thin stiff sapling: remove the bark and allow the wood to dry and stiffen for a couple of days. Attach a stretch of line the same length as the rod to the tip. Or improvise rings from wire and cast a longer line like a fly line.

Fish species and techniques vary widely

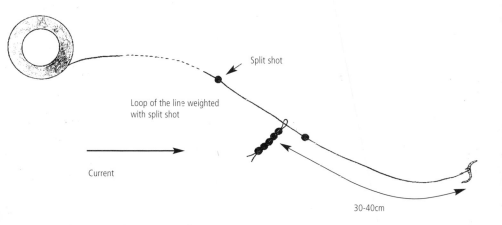

Split shot

Loop of the line weighted
with split shot

Current

30-40cm

Hand line and running ledger rig.

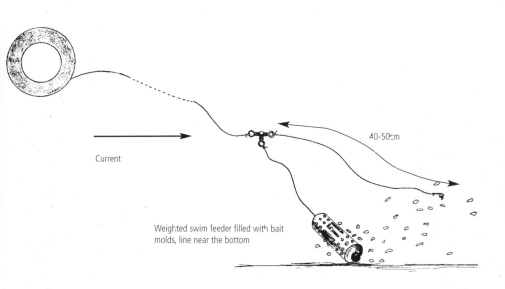

Current

40-50cm

Weighted swim feeder filled with bait
molds, line near the bottom

Hand line with fixed paternoster and swim feeder.

Lures - make sure you have a variety of lures, especially smaller sizes. A smaller fish won't take a big lure.

A small rod like this is ideal for wilderness travel.

around the globe. Before you enter any wild area ask local fishermen what tackle and bait they would use. If you cannot afford the weight of a rod in your outfit, try one of the following techniques.

Hand-line hobo fishing

Hand-line fishing offers less control than rod fishing, but it is rewarding in its simplicity. Many different sizes of fish can be caught in this way in both marine and inland waters. All manner of lures can be fished from a hand-line, but with a slower retrieve than that provided by geared lure fishing reels. I find that modern silicon-bodied jigs work best: they behave in a convincing way, even when retrieved slowly. But don't confine yourself to artificial lures: worm and hook are particularly effective on a hand-line when set as a simple fixed paternoster, or running leger. Let the line run over an outstretched finger to detect a bite.

One of the joys of hand-lining is its compactness: you do not need a purpose-made reel – virtually any smooth cylinder can be converted into a hand-line reel, and discarded beer cans or plastic drinks bottles are ideal. The latter provide a receptacle for tackle storage. I have even pressed a mosquito-repellent bottle into service as a hand-line reel. Attach the end of your line to your improvised reel then wind on the line by hand. Hold the reel securely in one hand, pointing it to where you intend the lure to fall. Cast the lure with the other hand in one smooth underhand swing, releasing it at just above waist height. With a few minutes' practice you will discover how economical a cast this is, and that you can place the lure with great accuracy. Retrieve the lure by winding the line on to the reel, staying alert to the vibrations caused by fish nibbling it. When a fish strikes, play him from the reel rather than your hand as you reel in.

Night-lines and trot lines

Night-lines are strictly prohibited in most circumstances, but in the wild they remain an effective emergency fishing method. Take a long length of heavy fishing line or thin nylon cord, attach dropper loops 30cm apart, and to each loop a leader of nylon line 40–50cm long. Tie on the hooks and bait them with thick leathery-skinned grubs and slugs rather than worms, which many fish can remove from the hook. Attach a rock at one end of the line and tie the other end to a thin flexible sapling or overhanging branch on shore. Lay the hooks and line into the water then cast out the rock from the bank. This will prevent tangling – and you hooking yourself. Once set, the night-line will fish many levels within the water. Check morning and evening, rebaiting and setting as necessary. Night-lines need not be large and cumbersome: 4–5-hook lines are fine.

In marine environments you can make a similar arrangement, but peg it to the seabed at low tide and retrieve it at the next low tide. Sandy areas among rock outcrops can be excellent places to catch flounders, dabs or plaice – bait with lugworm, limpet or fish.

Metal fish hooks are difficult to replace, but you can make do without them. Until the turn of the century trot-lines were set on sandbars in the Thames estuary with hooks made from hawthorn. Perhaps the most commonly employed alternative is the gorge hook, a toggle that turns side on and embeds itself in the throat or mouth of the fish. These can be made from bone, antler or even hard wood. Hooks almost identical to modern metal hooks were once carved from bone, and perhaps the most cunning hook I have ever seen was fashioned by Stone Age fishermen in what is now France from a wild-boar tusk which, in cross-section, has a perfect hook shape. In the far north of Europe a three-pronged Y-shaped gorge was still commonly used for catching burbot until recent times.

In the wilderness a gill net is a useful survival tool for emergencies.

On the Pacific coast of British Columbia and Alaska, the first nations fashioned a wide variety of specialised hooks from wood and bone. Their steam-bent and halibut hooks were works of art, but the trolling hook, made from wood, bone and lashed with a split root, is easily made and can be used to great effect in place of metal hooks.

Snaring

In clear water poachers snared fish. They cut a hazel or alder sapling to the required length, leaving the bark on, and attached a single strand of snare wire to the point with a noose 15cm in diameter. Often the wire was blackened with soot from a candle flame or a piece of birch bark. Then they lowered the snare into the water and carefully manoeuvred it over the fish's head and back behind the gill flap. Then they lifted it smartly upwards, bringing the fish into the air and to shore.

Netting

Unsporting and outlawed in managed waterways, the most important of all fishing techniques for survival in a remote land is the use of a gill net. Using this technique, you can take fish that are difficult to hook. A gill net is not heavy and takes up little space, so it is easy to bury one in your outfit. Traditionally native people used natural fibre nets dyed red, a tradition that survives today among northern net fishermen because red is difficult to see under water. I have set a gill net several times to discover it had caught fish before I had finished laying it.

Ice fishing

In winter, lakes and rivers in the far north freeze and the ice thickens progressively as the season deepens. Despite its apparent beauty, water in its frozen forms of snow and ice must at all times be considered treacherous. Moving on frozen water is hazardous at the beginning and end of winter and wherever the water is travelling fast over rapids or through narrows. I remember travelling one February for several hours by snowmobile over frozen lakes in

Labrador when my guide stopped to show me fast-moving water boiling up from an area clear of ice. In darkness or poor visibility and without his expert local knowledge, it would have been easy to drive straight into the water. Generally, the minimum thickness of freshwater ice that will support a single person on skis is 5cm, and it is as well to avoid moving on such thin ice. Bear in mind that a heavy snowfall on ice will load and stress it, as will a drop of the supporting water level below it. With ice 20cm thick, fishing is a far safer proposition. Frequently in midwinter ice can be a metre thick or more.

To break through ice, you will need either an ice chisel or an ice auger. With both tools, you must take great care not to injure your feet when using them.

Ice chisels are heavy and long-handled. The tip is either chisel-shaped, about 5cm wide, or triangularly pointed. The chisel-ended ones cut more efficiently but are more difficult to keep sharp and in good order than the triangular type. Widely used in Canada, they have no moving part to malfunction and will cut through very thick ice or cut very wide holes. On Baffin Island I have helped Inuit fishermen cut two holes through 2.5 metres of ice to set a net for Arctic char. It was a long and labour-intensive process.

In northern Europe, and increasingly elsewhere, rotary ice augers are preferred. Sometimes these are motorised and wide-bladed, but more commonly hand-powered. Fitted with two simple cutting blades they drill neatly through ice up to a metre thick. They are prone to damage from misuse, particularly if they are banged down on the ice, which blunts the blades. Like all sharp tools, ice chisels and augers should be either masked or set into the ice when not in use.

To cut through the ice, first clear an area of snow to expose the ice surface, then cut the hole. Once cut, the water will gush up so beware of soaking your feet. Clear any lumps of ice from the hole and shovel them away. Almost as soon as you have done this the surface of the water will begin to freeze over – keep it clear

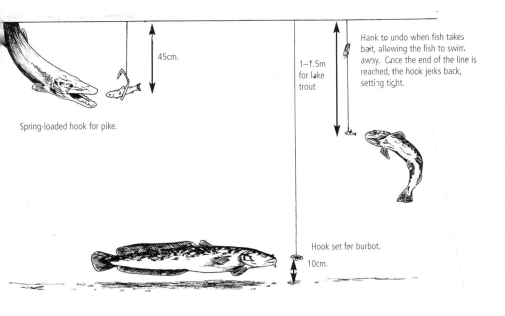

45cm.

Spring-loaded hook for pike.

1–1.5m for lake trout.

Hank to undo when fish takes bait, allowing the fish to swim away. Once the end of the line is reached, the hook jerks back, setting tight.

Hook set for burbot.

10cm.

①

②

③

Using a stick will enable you to chip out the line if the hole freezes closed, without fear of cutting the line and losing both fish and tackle.

Mark the location of the hole, so that it can be found after snowfall.

by scooping away the ice. Ice fishermen use special scoops but the tip of a snow shovel does equally well.

Indigenous people usually fish through ice with a short stick or rod, and metal lures. They place spruce boughs, a reindeer or caribou pelt beneath their knees for insulation. However, I opt for a set-line left overnight. In this hooks can be baited, increasing the prospect of a catch. Ensure that your line is in the centre of the hole to prevent it being frozen in as the hole will refreeze inwards from the edge. Then plug the hole opening with some spruce-bough tips and cover it well with snow as insulation to slow the freezing process. If you attach the line to an anchor stick longer than your knife blade you will be able to reopen the hole, should it freeze, by chipping without fear of cutting the line.

Eels

Eels were once caught widely for food by workers in the British countryside, and to this day eels and liquor – a type of gravy – are

popular in the East End of London. Both freshwater and marine eels are edible but avoid the large tropical marine eels found in coral reefs as they may be toxic.

Eel grabbing
The simplest method of catching eels is to pluck them from clear, shallow water. As with all things bushcraft, simple is not necessarily easy – rare indeed is the countryman who is well accomplished in this technique. To grasp an eel, lock it in a scissor grip between your middle, index and third fingers, hooking the middle finger over the eel.

Eel line
Eels can be caught with hook and line, and commonly with a night-line anchored at the bank to a thin sapling or, more traditionally, a tied-back branch that acted as a shock absorber, preventing the eel breaking the line.

Opposite page: Ice fishing

Babbing, freshwater and marine eels

For freshwater eels: thread a length of wool through a mass of worms and tie it into a loop so that the worms are squeezed together. Attach the loop to a stronger line, then to a sapling rod. Let the worms drift down with the current in a stream or ditch towards where you have seen an eel or suspect it to be. When the eel takes the bait the wool becomes entangled in its needle-like teeth. Pull the eel upward – steadily so it cannot escape.

An alternative method involves placing the bait – rank-smelling animal intestine is ideal – in a small bag woven from thin fibrous material; onion sacks and hairnets are popular.

Eel bag

A reliable means of taking eels. You will need a cloth sack and some suitable bait, such as high-smelling intestine. Weight the sack with a small rock, half fill it with dry grass or similar and place the bait in the middle. Close the bag and cut some small slits in its side. These should be large enough only to encourage the eel to bite its way into the sack. Attach a line to the sack and throw it into a deep pool. Leave it overnight and retrieve it early in the morning. With luck you will find one or more eels inside.

Eel gaffs and spears

Perhaps the most widespread means of taking eels.

Eel traps and boxes, freshwater and marine

Traps range from simple bamboo tubes to elegantly woven wicker baskets, but today eel baskets are made from wire mesh. An interesting marine eel trap I saw in Western Samoa consisted of a wooden box with a round opening. On the inside a tin fitted with a cloth sleeve formed a tunnel entrance. When the eel entered the box through the sleeve it could not find the way out again. The trap was baited with a dead fish then buried in the side of a coral head and left overnight. The tin-can/sleeve tunnel can also be used with a sack instead of a box.

MAMMALS

In our pre-farming past, trapping was the easiest way to secure meat. It is an important and effective survival skill. Unfortunately, in the past we have allowed indiscriminate trapping skills to bring some species to the brink of extinction or beyond it. For traditional trappers, respect and wisdom of generations dictate the method and quota to be taken on trap lines. Employ techniques that are effective yet minimise suffering, and only use them in times of need.

Rabbit snares

An ancient means of trapping, which is still in relatively widespread usage today. The traditional British rabbit snare comprised four parts: the snare itself, ideally made from

Modern British rabbit snare.

Hare snare set in the Arctic.

six–eight strands of thin brass wire with a free running eyelet twisted in; the cord; the teeler stick and the peg or stake. The snares are placed on a rabbit trail over the low place where the rabbit lands when moving down the trail. Snares can also be placed on the rabbits' look-out post, but never at a burrow entrance. Traditionally the snare was set with a noose of fist size diameter held four fingers high by a teeler stick made from a short cleft of hazel wand. The cord was then staked firmly to the ground. Today a modified snare is more commonly employed incorporating a teeler of fencing wire to which the wire is firmly anchored, the cord and peg being made fast to a loop in the wire teeler. The wire of

these newer snares is set at the same height but with a larger diameter loop.

The same arrangement is frequently used for taking hares but the noose is pear-shaped and set hand-high on the run.

Rabbits and hares taken by these means are usually alive when the snares are checked, sitting quietly. The trapper dispatches the rabbit without fuss or alarm by gently grasping its neck between two fingers of one hand and the hind feet with the other. Then, with a smart, firm, stretching action, he breaks its neck with a simultaneous deft lifting of the rabbit's chin. Done correctly, this is the most humane and certain way to dispatch a rabbit.

ACKNOWLEDGEMENTS

A dear friend once told me that writing a book is like being pregnant, and this book has been no exception. While publishers paced the corridors of Hodder & Stoughton eager for news of the expected arrival, friends and colleagues proffered advice and support; they are owed the greatest debt of gratitude. Thanks then to the Woodlore team, particularly Ben McNutt who has provided all of the illustrations for Bushcraft. Also to Juha Rankinen and James Lock for demonstrating for the camera. To Tom Lutyens, the ablest of US Survival Instructors, for demonstrating banana craft, and to Eleanor Dunn for helping with setting up photos and carrying camera bags. Also to Ian Palmer, whose hands make a brief appearance in Fire.

Special thanks must go to: Gordon Hillman for his unflinching support and advice, Rob and Barbara Newington for providing locations for much of the photography, Lord and Lady Selborne and Viscount Chelsea for believing in the value of bushcraft.

To true friends and men who really know the woods – Lars Fält, Robert Colin-Stokes, George Neal and Peter Nicol, and to the many different indigenous peoples who have invited me to their firesides and showed me the way that they employ bushcraft.

To Jane Brown for typing the manuscript, and the greatest thanks of all to Rachel, without whose strength this book would never have been completed.

All photographs by the author, except: page 50 Tom Lutyens; page 64 top left and bottom right Danny Cane; pages 126 and 146 Barrie Foster. From Oxford Scientific Films (OSF): page 192 top left Bob Gibbons; pages 192 bottom right, 195 centre, 204, 205 top left and centre G.A. Maclean; pages 194 top, 201 bottom left Barrie E. Watts; page 194 top Mike Slater; pages 195 middle right and bottom right Ian West; page 196 top left Niall Benvie, top centre LSF; page 196 centre Faithjof Skibbe, middle right Tim Shepherd; page 201 middle H.L. Fox; page 206 top centre Sinclair Stammers, top right Bob Fredrick; page 208 Laurence Gould; page 204 top right and top left G.I. Bernard, top centre Fredrick Ehrenstrom; page 201 bottom C.W. Helliwell. From Nature Library: page 205 bottom left Brian Lightfoot.

PHOTOGRAPHY

Throughout Bushcraft the photographs were taken using Fuji film. For the most part they have been taken on Provia 100 or 100F although, where practical, Velvia has been used and, where necessary, Provia 400 and 400F.

All of the 35mm images were captured with Nikon cameras and lenses, mostly using FM2 or F5.

Panoramic images were taken on a Hasselblad X-Pan, and medium format images on a Hasselblad 203FE.

INDEX